The Complete Beginner's Guide to Ice Skating

The Complete Beginner's Guide to ICE SKATING

EDWARD F. DOLAN, JR.

Doubleday & Company, Inc.   Garden City, New York

Library of Congress Cataloging in Publication Data

Dolan, Edward F   1924–
   The complete beginner's guide to ice skating.

   SUMMARY: This beginner's guide to ice skating includes chapters on the first time on ice, ice safety, skating backward, curving, circles, figure skating, and other techniques.
      1. Skating—Juvenile literature. [1. Ice skating]
   I. Title.
GV849.D64   1974   796.9′1
ISBN 0-385-01682-4 Trade
        0-385-03779-1 Prebound
Library of Congress Catalog Card Number 73–10803

This book is for Rose

Acknowledgments

For much fine assistance and cooperation in the preparation of this book, I am much in the debt of: the personnel at *Raydine Ice Skating*, Corte Madera, California, especially Ray Schramm and Miss Hetti Schramm; skaters Wendy Abbett, Mike Chadwick, and Bob Fleming; and photographer James Stewart.

Contents

The Complete Beginner's Guide to Ice Skating

ONE

Let's Go Skating

Did you ever think about taking up ice skating as a hobby?

And did you then quickly put the whole idea aside after watching an Olympics star or a hockey great perform on television? Did you shake your head and mutter, "I'll never be able to do *that!*"?

Your discouragement was quite normal. It has stung many another young person sitting there in front of a TV set. But you made a mistake in letting it get you down, for it then kept you from trying a sport that never fails to excite and please.

So be discouraged no more. The facts of the matter are that ice skating is a sport *easy to enter* and *not difficult to learn.* It has room for all degrees of ability and offers *more varieties of recreational fun* than most any other sport you can think of. You need not be hockey's Bobby Hull, or Janet Lynn of Olympics fame, to enjoy yourself thoroughly.

But wait a minute. Is it really a sport easy to enter?

You bet it is. You don't have to be of any special physical build before you dare go near the ice. Not important is the tallness required for basketball, the muscles demanded in football, the "batting eye" and "golden glove" called for in baseball, or the fleetness loved by all track coaches. You can be tall, short, thin, or chubby. You can be as smart as the proverbial whip or a little on the dense side. You can wear glasses, have big feet or small feet, and be knock-kneed or bowlegged. Nothing counts against you. Ice skating will make room for you.

It can all be summed up in one instructor's remark: "If you have a normal sense of balance and can walk, you can become an ice skater."

Now, what about the claim that ice skating is not difficult to learn? Is that, honestly, true?

Try this for an answer: It is not unusual to see two- and three-year-old children starting to make their way around a rink and soon coming to do so with ease and skill. Nor especially unusual to see people in their sixties donning skates for the first time; in some areas, senior citizen groups get together to form skating classes. Even certain of the handicapped are able to participate; blind children, for instance, often take lessons and are able to glide over the ice with a minimum of assistance.

And, in the span of years that divide the very young from the elderly, you'll see people from every walk of life at an ice rink— everyone from students and housewives to lawyers, doctors, and engineers. Just name the profession and you'll find it represented. And look for whole families skating together. Even in this era of the "generation gap," they'll be there in goodly number.

Altogether, in our country, ice skating claims some thirty million active participants. It simply could not appeal to so many people were it especially difficult to learn.

But make no mistake. It is not so easy that it will bore you. Right from your first day at the rink, it will challenge your balance, your concentration, your coordination, and your muscular strength. The challenges will grow as you develop your skill and advance to the more difficult skating movements. But they will be exciting challenges, and you will feel a deep satisfaction and pleasure as each is mastered.

And, of course, you may accept only as many of the challenges as you wish. On the one hand, you may be perfectly happy just skating easily along for the rest of your life and knowing no more than how to curve around in the opposite direction when you come to the end of the rink. On the other, you may decide to become a championship skater, perhaps the best in the world. Either goal is just fine. The important thing is that you do what you want to do—and that you have a whopping good time while doing it.

Now for the claim that ice skating offers a wider variety of activities than most other sports. Is that an exaggeration?

Indeed not. When you play a game such as football, basketball, or handball, you play just one game. When you play tennis, you may alternate between singles and doubles, and between hard and grass courts—but the game remains essentially the same. In contrast, just look at the following skating possibilities:

1. Would you like to spend a few hours a week gliding smoothly around a rink, enjoying the company of fellow enthusiasts, attempting various ice maneuvers, and benefiting from all the fine exercise? Try general, or recreational, skating.

2. Are you interested in a competitive sport, one in which you can win as much recognition as your local quarterback or pitcher? One that is without the violence that keeps so many young people away from the body-contact sports? One that, in time and with enough practice, may lead to a national, an international, or an Olympics championship? Or to a career as an instructor or a professional ice-show skater? Try competitive figure skating.

3. Or do you like body-contact sports? Do you want competition that is fast and fierce? Try ice hockey.

4. Or is it racing that you like? Would you enjoy pitting yourself against a stopwatch, or a competitor, and cranking yourself up to speeds of twenty-five and thirty miles an hour—speeds said to be among the fastest that man can achieve on his two feet? Try speed skating.

5. And what if music is your pleasure? Do you like to dance? Would you like to skate as much as possible with a special someone? Try either pairs skating or ice dancing.

Something for everybody. That's the motto for ice skating.

Should you decide that here's exactly the sport you've been

looking for, you will find that you were born at just the right time to enjoy it to the fullest. Everything has been developed to its best for you—the equipment, the skating techniques, and the facilities. Hundreds of years have gone into that development.

No one knows exactly when early man stumbled upon the idea that he could skate on ice. The first traces of the sport are to be found in the Scandinavian countries of about two thousand years ago. There, so written records tell us, men made their way along frozen streams with the aid of animal bones strapped to their feet. Much used were the rib and shank bones of the elk, the reindeer, and the ox. Had you lived at that time, you would have made your skates by grinding the bones to a smooth finish after sawing away their bulging ends.

Skating, of course, was anything but graceful and easy on such primitive contrivances. Yet it must have pleased people, for it spread from country to country as the centuries passed. In Siberia, the people learned to get about on walrus tusks. In China, cornstalks were tried for a time. By the twelfth century, the sport was widespread in England. A British writer had this to say of it:

"When the great fenne or moore is frozen, many young men play on the yce. . . . Some tye bones to their feet and under their heeles, and shoving themselves by a little picked staffe, do slide as swiftly as a bird flyeth in the aire, or an arrow out of a crossbow."

Though much enjoyed wherever it went in Europe, skating found its greatest popularity in Holland. There, it was not only a pleasant fresh-air pastime but an important means of transportation. Several Dutch paintings of the fourteenth century are filled with figures scooting along the canals that run through the country and become frozen highways in the winter. Certain of the figures are obviously skating for the sheer fun of it. But others are on their way to work or are hauling goods to or from market.

If you look closely at the figures, you will see that they have actual skates tied to their feet—wooden skates that gripped the ice far better than did the animal bones of old. In the late eighteenth century, an even firmer grip was to be had when the first iron skates were manufactured and lashed to the feet with leather straps. Then, in the nineteenth century, the straps were replaced by a device that clamped the skate to the shoe. So far as most skaters were concerned, this last invention was the best of all. The leather straps were clumsy to wear and had the bad habit of loosening after a few minutes of activity. Now the skates were securely locked in place.

All these improvements opened the way to the various kinds of skating that we enjoy today. Ice games and races had always been popular, but, with every improvement in skate design, they became more popular and began to be formalized. Ice clubs were formed in England and elsewhere for racing according to strict rules; speed skating as we know it was born. In the Canada of the 1860s, a group of imaginative British soldiers transferred the age-old game of field hockey to a frozen pond; ice hockey came into being, with its first set of formal rules to follow in a few years. At the very same time, the general skating public was beginning to devise simple patterns that could be traced on the ice. The first attempts at figure skating were being made.

Were you to go back to the last century, you would find the figure skating of the day odd and stilted by modern standards. The back was held straight and stiff in some countries, bent forward and stiff in others. The arms were folded across the chest. Ladies skated quite daintily, with their blades often hidden beneath voluminous skirts. Gentlemen glided along boldly, stocking caps flying.

It was an American dancing teacher, Jackson Haines, who finally put all the stiffness to flight. While living in Europe during the 1860s, he applied certain dance techniques to skating and developed a style that sent a skater gliding through his various patterns and maneuvers with a flowing grace and freedom. Haines' style caught on throughout Europe and, in time, swept the United States. Out of it, with new patterns and movements being added through the years, came today's figure skating and its two first cousins, ice dancing and pairs skating.

Though ice skating has always been a favorite activity in countries where the winters are bitter, its popularity in centuries past could never match the widespread approval that it has won in our day and age. In this twentieth century, it is a worldwide favorite. It is in this happy position thanks to several developments.

First, steel blades came into broad use in the twentieth century after being first manufactured in the late 1800s; light in weight and with a fine gripping power when properly sharpened, they made skating more of a pleasure than ever before. Second, the clamps were put aside in favor of blades and boots fastened together by means of screws; again, greater pleasure for the skater, for now he could truly feel secure on his feet. Third, ice skating made countless new fans through the Olympics and then the appearances of such champions as Sonja Henie in motion pictures and traveling ice shows. Thousands of people who had never thought of ice skating as a hobby decided to give it a try. Then came television's coverage of the Olympics and other international meets. The result: even more new enthusiasts.

But there is little doubt that the most important development of all has been the modern indoor ice rink. By itself, it could not help but attract people to skating. It has brought the sport to all those areas that never see a snowy day. It has made skating safer than ever before by freezing the ice to a solid consistency; no longer need the skater worry about falling through the weak spots that plague all outdoor ice. And it has made skating possible in all seasons and at all hours. You need now never hang up your skates when spring comes or when darkness falls on your neighborhood pond or stream.

Top equipment. Flowing and graceful ways of getting around the ice. The finest facilities. After centuries of development, this is what skating means to today's participant. All can be yours. All you need do is slip into a pair of skates and step out on the ice.

Sounds too good to pass up, doesn't it?

This book is being written to help you enjoy and take part in your new sport to the fullest, no matter whether you intend the simplest of general skating or already have your eye on hockey stardom, a racing championship, or an Olympics gold medal for figure skating. The book will move along with you a step at a time toward your goal, beginning with your equipment and turning from there to the most fundamental of the basics of skating. Then through the more advanced fundamentals we'll go until we're talking about all the varieties of top skating possible—from figure work to racing and hockey.

Only one thing remains to be said before we start:

Good luck and good fun to you.

TWO

The Tools of Skating

If you've talked to a friend who has tried his hand at the sport, you already know that skating requires little equipment. You need not bother yourself with all the rods and reels cherished by the fisherman, nor with the cameras, lenses, light meters, and filters carried by the nature photographer. Aside from comfortable leisure-time clothing, you need only three items: the skates themselves, a pair of skate guards, and a tote bag for your gear.

Further, unlike many another sportsman, you need not purchase any equipment right away. During your first days on the ice, you can use "house equipment"—skates provided by the rink for a small rental fee. In fact, you *should* use rentals in the beginning so that, before ever breaking into your savings account, you can give yourself the chance to learn whether you are really going to enjoy skating. Once you find out, then it will be time to think about skates of your own.

But, even while you are still using rentals, you should become thoroughly acquainted with the tools of skating, especially with the skates themselves. As in all activities, you cannot hope for mastery until you know your equipment and what it will do for you.

So let's start that get-acquainted period right now.

Your Skates

In centuries past, when the runners were tied or clamped to the feet, the term "skates" referred just to the blades alone, but now it usually includes both the blades and the boots. Three types of skates have been developed over the years for use on the ice, each differing from the others in construction. Each is named after the activity for which it is designed: the *figure skate,* the *speed* (or *racing*) *skate,* and the *hockey skate.*

The figure skate is the most widely used of the trio. While its hockey and speed cousins are intended principally for their sports alone, it is the choice of the general skater as well as the figure skater. Thanks to its design, it is as versatile a skate as you will ever find. At one extreme, it will carry you smoothly around the rink at varying speeds or serve you well in informal ice games. At the other, it will permit you to execute intricate figure maneuvers that would prove unduly difficult or downright impossible on either the hockey or the speed blade.

But what if your ultimate goal is racing or hockey? Even then, the figure skate cannot be overlooked, for it is the one on which all first training should be given. It is advised for training on a number

THE FIGURE SKATE

of counts, among them the fact that its blade sets you closer to the ice than does the hockey blade and thus helps to overcome the tendency of the ankle to bend inward, a problem that troubles practically every learner for a time.

Because it is recommended for training and is so much used in general skating, we must—now and in forthcoming chapters—give the lion's share of attention to the figure skate. If you are especially interested in racing or hockey, please be patient until we reach the chapter titled "For Fun and Competition: Variety on Ice." There you will find descriptions of their skates.

For anyone who has ever visited an ice show or watched the Olympics on television, the figure skate is a familiar sight. It can be immediately identified, even at a distance, by the pronounced height of its leather boot. While hockey and speed boots end at ankle level, the figure boot rises to about the point where the calf muscles begin to bulge at the back of the leg. From sole to top, it measures about nine inches for boys and around eight inches for girls. Traditionally, the girl's boot is white, the boy's black.

As for the blade, it is quite as distinctive as the boot. Fashioned of steel, it juts out about two inches behind the boot heel and extends an inch or so beyond the toe. Up front, it describes a graceful curve from the ice to the boot tip. Cut into the lower part of the curve is a set of tiny notches called *toe picks* or *toe rakes*. They are needed to grip the ice during certain of the jumps, spins, and stops performed in figure skating.

Not only the curve but two stanchions rise from the blade to the boot. All are welded to two steel plates: the curve and the front stanchion to the *sole plate,* and the rear stanchion to the *heel plate.* Screws inserted through holes in the plates fasten the blade and boot together, binding them into a single, compact unit. When you finally get up on your skates, you will be about three inches off the ice.

On its underside, the blade measures a little less than a quarter inch wide. It surprises most beginners to learn that the blade is not flat across this narrow span. Rather, the steel is hollowed out so that a convex-shaped groove runs the full length of the blade and

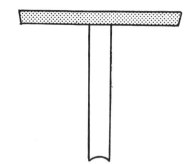

BLADE HOLLOW AND EDGES

gives it two distinct edges. Thanks to these edges, many a skater argues that he is not gliding along on just two blades but actually on four.

The edges are a figure skating "must," for they enable you to grip the ice firmly. Without them, your blade will always tend to skid as you curve, circle, or change direction. With them, you are able to sail through the most demanding maneuvers. Actually, the expert skater spends the bulk of his time on his blade edges, for most figure skating consists of curving and circling movements, and they cannot be easily performed with the blade flat on the ice. One edge or the other must be used if the skater is to veer away from a straight-line path.

So important are the edges that skaters long ago gave them names: *inside edge* for the one along the arch side of the foot, ·*outside edge* for its companion opposite. They are terms that you will find yourself needing to use every time you skate, especially if you take the sport seriously and advance to figure work.

Now, a final point in our introduction to the figure skate: Just as the underside of the blade is not flat across its width, so is it not built in a straight line from front to back. Rather, it is cut in a rocking-chair curve called the *radius*. The curve is a slight one, so slight that, were you not looking for it, the odds are that it would escape your notice. But, along with the edges, it is the feature most responsible for making the figure blade work as it does.

Why? A blade that is flat along its length—as is many a racing blade—will develop a great deal of straight-line speed and carry you around the wide turns in an oval track, but it is not meant for the sudden and repeated changes of direction demanded in figure skating, nor for all the curves and tight circles. Too much of the blade is always against the ice to make such maneuvers convenient or even possible. It is his blade radius—in combination with his edges—that enables the figure skater to perform as he does, gracefully and without breaking his neck. The less blade that there is to touch the ice at any one time, the easier it becomes to turn, curve, and alter direction.

The curve is fashioned so that it will fit at any point along the inside edge of an imaginary circle with a radius of approximately six feet.

Buying Skates of Your Own

While rental equipment will serve adequately for your first experiments on ice, you should not waste a moment in buying skates of your own once you decide to stick with the sport. By themselves, they will do much to hasten the development of your skills, for, if purchased with care, they will fit you exactly, with the boots giving your feet and ankles the best support possible. Though all rinks carry a wide range of sizes for their rental customers, you can only be guaranteed a truly good fit with skates of your own; too often, your foot may prove too narrow or too wide in spots for the rentals in stock. And you can skate well only if the boot fits properly and provides maximum support.

Skates may be purchased in one of two ways at the rink shop or a sporting goods store. You may buy the boots and blades separately and then have the dealer attach them. Or you may buy them in *matched sets*—that is, already fastened together. In either case, you should get the best-quality skates that you can afford, even if you have to stretch your pocketbook a little. Though they may cost more at the outset, quality skates will eventually prove to be an economical investment. They will give you long service and, considering the time you will spend on them, their cost will finally break down to just a few pennies an hour—a real bargain in this day and age.

If you plan to skate just for pleasure, you can buy a substantial pair of skates for around twenty-five dollars or so. More expensive skates will be needed should you decide to go on to figure work and competition. They will cost from a low of about fifty dollars to upward of a hundred dollars.

To be sure that you get your money's worth, buy your skates only from a dealer who knows something about ice skating, for only then will he be able to help you make the best selection possible. And, no matter how expert he is, be sure to lend him a hand by keeping the following points about boots and blades firmly in mind.

The Boot

The importance of a properly fitting boot cannot be over-emphasized. The boot, which should be made of durable leather, provides support for the foot and ankle, a job that it is helpless to do unless it fits well. Without proper fit, you can count on tired feet and wobbly ankles—and, as you'll see in a moment, on feet that bite far too much with the cold.

What is proper boot size? Many a beginner thinks that the boot should be a half to a full size larger than his regular shoe so that he can stuff a pair—or even two or three pairs—of heavy socks into it for warmth. He's 100 percent wrong. Depending on the shape of the foot, the best boot fit is a half to a full size *smaller* than your walking shoe. Only then, when it is laced, will the boot give you the support necessary for the rigors of skating. If your foot is extremely wide, however, you may be able to wear a boot that is the same size as your regular shoe.

But a half to full size too small! Isn't the boot likely to be uncomfortable? The answer is "Yes"—but the discomfort will not hang about for long. After a few skating sessions, the boot will mold itself to your foot, and will start, as experienced skaters say, "to feel as if it's a part of you." From then on, it will be of no bother.

When being fitted for the boot, wear lightweight socks or, if you're a girl, the tights that are a part of the traditional female skating costume. Do not wear one or more pairs of heavy socks—now or at any time on the ice. No matter what you may have heard, heavy socks will not keep the foot warm. They will fit into nothing but a too-large boot, which then has to be laced too tightly before it gives any impression of support. The tight lacing hinders the circulation in your foot and ankle, with the result that they soon grow colder than need be.

Proper boot fit involves more than a smaller-than-walking-shoe size. The boot must hold your heel, your instep, and your ankle snugly. To ensure correct heel fit, push your foot as deeply into the boot as you can and press down hard on the sole. You should then be able to slip your heel up and down only in the very slightest degree even when the boot is loosely laced.

Now check for tightness elsewhere. The boot must fit snugly throughout the instep and so, if all is well, you will find no wrinkles in the leather from the big-toe joint back to the heel. Likewise, the unwrinkled leather will run up to the ankle. Finally, lace the boot as you would when preparing for a practice session. There should be a space of about 1 to 1½ inches between the boot walls as they travel up the top of the foot and the front of the leg.

Only one part of the boot need not be snug: the toe area. There you must have sufficient room to flex and move the toes freely. The leather should not rub against or jam them together in any way. If the toes are at all pinched, the pressure exerted by the leather will soon cause them to ache and, interfering with proper circulation, will turn them intensely cold.

The Blade

As you know, boots and blades may be purchased separately or in matched sets. If you choose to buy them separately, don't hand over your money until you have made certain that the blades fit the boots and are then attached to them correctly.

To check for proper fit, simply hold each blade against the sole of its boot. The front of the sole plate should not extend beyond the tip of the boot, while the heel plate should rest squarely on the boot heel. Even if the salesman tempts you with the bargain price of the century, never settle for blades whose plates extend beyond either the boot tip or the heel. They will prove unfailingly clumsy.

If the blade is to be correctly attached (*mounted* is the skater's

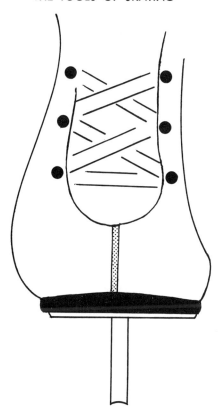

CORRECT BLADE SETTING

term), it should be placed so that it does not pass along the foot's exact midline. Insist that it be set slightly to the inside of the midline. For most beginners, the blade should run approximately between the big and second toe.

Why set the blade inside the midline? Your first few moments on the ice will give you the answer. Your ankles will wobble and tend to bend inward. Very quickly, you're apt to begin thinking, "I'll never learn how to do this. I bet I've got weak ankles."

The moan of "weak ankles" is the most often heard of beginner complaints. Actually, very few people have any such problem. Rather, wobble and bend come of attempting to balance yourself for the first time on two thin strips of steel. All the trouble is significantly reduced when the blade is placed not along the foot's exact midline but to the inside of it.

For most skaters, the blade needs to be set just slightly to the inside. But some skaters, thanks to their physical builds, must have the blade mounted at some point farther in from the midline before it will work satisfactorily. You may be one of them and, if so, do not be concerned if several resettings are necessary before the correct one is found. The resettings, incidentally, will not damage the sole of the boot, for the rink shop will plug up each set of old screw holes before making new ones.

Should you buy your skates in a matched set, you will have to keep the idea of possible resettings uppermost in mind. There should be no problem if the blades are premounted with screws, but you may be in for some trouble if, as is the case with some matched sets, they are riveted into place. The job of removing rivets may prove to be a difficult one, which will perhaps scar the boot sole. If you know, however, that resetting is not going to be required, then there are on the market many riveted skates (they often cost a little less than screw-mounted pairs) that will serve you well.

Skate Guards and Tote Bag

If you begin your skating under an instructor, you will certainly be no more than a few minutes into your first lesson before you hear him say, "Your skates are for skating on the ice. Don't wear them anywhere else. If you must walk around in them, be sure to put on skate guards."

Skate guards are slender containers that are about three inches longer than the blades themselves. Each guard has a slit running down its middle into which the blade is inserted and then held in place by means of a spring device. Any skater will agree that the guards are the blades' best friends, for they provide protection against all the off-ice bumps and scrapes that can quickly dull the edges and knick or chip even the best of steel.

The instructor is exaggerating a little when he tells you to uncover your blades only when you are on the ice. You can also walk with bare blades on the rubber matting that surrounds the rink and runs to the dressing area; the matting is intended to protect the blades and to save you the inconvenience of donning guards

Skate Guards

every time you leave the ice. But walk nowhere else without them.

All extra walking, even on soft carpeting, unnecessarily dulls the edges, while every hard or dirty surface that you can think of threatens damage to the exposed blade. Do not trot guardless across the wood floor to the rink shop or the soft-drink stand. And *definitely* do not walk across the sidewalk to the family car, or, as many a beginner on the young side has been known to do, make your way down the street and around a couple of corners to your home; nothing is as dangerous as concrete to the bare blade. And, at home, don't test your balance on the brick patio or pose on the tile floor in front of the bathroom mirror.

Guards are manufactured in wood, plastic, or rubber. They can be purchased quite inexpensively. Some new sets cost as little as two dollars, while used pairs can be obtained at the rink shop for under a dollar.

Equally inexpensive in most cases is the tote bag. If you wish, you can purchase canvas or leatherette bags in the shape of your skates for as little as three to five dollars. Otherwise, along with so many skaters, you may simply carry your skates about in a canvas airline carrier or an overnight case.

Incidentally, it's a good idea to write your name in indelible ink on your guards and your tote bag so that they will not be confused with all the other guards and bags always to be found in the dressing area.

CLOTHING

Neither expensive nor fancy clothes are required for skating. You may one day decide to buy or make a skating costume, but in the meantime, all that is needed is an ordinary leisure-time outfit. It must, however, be comfortable and trim. Comfort is absolutely necessary if you are to be free to concentrate fully on learning the skills of skating. Trimness is a "must" if you are to have that graceful look that is the hallmark of all fine skaters.

For comfort, your skating clothes should be warm, but not so bulky as to interfere with your movements. Slacks in combination with pullover sweaters, windbreakers, jackets, or shirts (blouses for the girls) are fine. Depending on how chilly the rink is, winter underwear—even insulated—can be added. Boys should wear lightweight wool or cotton socks, while girls may choose socks, panty hose, or tights. Additionally, girls may wear some sort of head covering—perhaps a scarf or a cap—but not a wide-brimmed, floppy hat. In many areas, the old tradition that it is impolite for boys to wear headgear in an enclosed rink is still observed.

Though your clothing must always be trim, it must also be sufficiently roomy. It is impossible to learn and perfect a skating maneuver while your outfit is binding you painfully under the arms or about the legs. Girls should avoid the floor-length dresses so much in vogue today; as attractive as they may look, they promise only to snag on the skates. Likewise, street dresses or skirts should not be worn to the rink. The anticipated embarrassment of skirt and slip flying in all directions in the event of a fall is bound to interfere with your concentration.

The rules of trimness are the same for the ice as anywhere else. Always keep your shirt or blouse neatly tucked in. Take care that the colors of your outfit blend or match. Be certain that your clothing is always clean. You simply cannot achieve a look of grace with blouse bunched at the waist, shirttail flying, or slacks wrinkled and soiled.

As your skill improves, you may want a costume for pleasure skating, and assuredly so if you enter figure or dance competition. The choice here is traditional for girls. The costume consists of skin-colored tights, a skating dress or skirt, and pants. If you select a skirt rather than a dress, it can be worn with a sweater or blouse. By itself or as part of a dress, the skirt should always be short, full, and flared from the hipline. It may be either circular, gored, or pleated. Some skaters feel that the pants should be the same color as the skirt so that undue attention will not be attracted to your behind.

You may make your own costume, but you will find that many sporting goods stores carry a wide range of costumes, most of them very reasonably priced. You may add decorative touches of jewelry —sequins, clips, earrings, and hair adornments. You will be wise, however, to keep jewelry at a minimum. Extravagantly applied, it can give you a "bits and pieces" look and detract from your graceful appearance.

The costume possibilities for boys are wider. They range from slacks and sweater or shirt to a tuxedo or a full-dress suit. Costume components may be matched, blended, or contrasted in color. When selecting a costume, your chief aim will be to decide on the type of outfit most appropriate for your general appearance and your type of skating.

There. We've talked about all the equipment necessary for skating. Now let's get to the rink and see how you're going to do on the ice itself.

THREE

The Basics: First Time on the Ice

The big moment is *now*. Clutching your skates, you approach the ice. In another few moments, you'll be giving the sport that has long been called an art your first try.

Your emotions are no doubt mixed. You're excited, eager to see how well you're going to do, but at the same time you're hesitant, even a little frightened. You know full well that you're going to end up sitting or sprawled on the ice before the day is done. The falls are not going to hurt too much, but your ego is bound to suffer. For everywhere there are other skaters, all of them gliding confidently along as though they were born on their blades. You're certain that you're going to look foolish and draw amused glances all around.

Right now, let's put that fear in its proper place, for, if you allow it to bother you too much, it will interfere with the development of your skating skills and may even drive you to give up the sport altogether. Indeed, you're going to slip, slide, wave your arms helplessly, and fall. And, yes, the surrounding skaters are going to grin. But you can be sure of one thing: The grins will be sympathetic and understanding. Every skater out there has suffered through the comic clumsiness that always accompanies first learning. Every skater has taken his fair share of tumbles. And every skater knows the problems you'll soon be facing and striving to overcome. No one is going to think you a clumsy fool.

The fact is that you will earn only a few smiles—and for just a few moments. Your fellow skaters will be too busy perfecting their own skills, or too busy having a good time, to give your wobbles and slips more than passing notice. They'll recognize you as a beginner and let it go at that, knowing that the day will come when you'll be as confident on your blades as they are on theirs. And you can bet that you'll soon have several experienced skaters gliding over to get acquainted and to cheer you on with a few bits of advice.

So carry on. Be clumsy. Who cares?

GETTING READY FOR THE ICE

Having set aside any fears about bruising your ego, let's get ready for the ice. Slip into your boots, pushing your feet deep into them and settling your heels firmly in the heel sections. Now, regardless of your excitement, take the time to lace the boots correctly.

For boots to be properly laced, you should leave the thongs somewhat loose in the eyelets from the toe to about the instep bone. From the instep bone to the first or second eyelet above the ankle bone, pull the thongs as *tightly as possible*. Then, for the rest of the way to the boot top, again leave them snug but a bit on the loose side.

With each boot laced in this fashion, you will give your toes ample freedom for easy movement and will allow for sufficient blood circulation at the boottop. The area of tight lacing in between will securely encase your foot and ankle in leather, providing them with the best support possible.

Once the lacings are tied off, be sure to tuck their ends into the boottops. A trailing thong that finds its way beneath your blade means a sure tumble.

Now you're ready to skate. If you are with an instructor, he will introduce you to the ice and tell you of the precautions you now must exercise. If you are by yourself, you should learn these precautions on your own before ever leaving the sidelines. They are necessary not only for your own welfare but for that of your fellow skaters.

You're going to be on a slippery and unfamiliar surface, and so resist all temptation to "fool around," for you're bound to end up sitting on the ice. Without an instructor, you will not be in an area reserved for learners and safely away from general rink traffic. For the time being, do your best to stay clear of the surrounding skaters, at the same time keeping a sharp eye out for them. If you skitter or wander absent-mindedly into another's path, you'll both likely go down in a heap. Skating is one of the safest of sports, but it does require courtesy and caution on the parts of all. If you use your common sense, all will be well.

ON THE ICE

Actually, unless you are foolishly daring, you will automatically approach the ice with due caution and not challenge the fates by plunging out from the sidelines to see how far your flailing arms and thrashing feet will carry you. You will undoubtedly grip the *boards* (the skater's term for the barrier or handrail bordering the ice) and, somewhat as if testing the water in a swimming pool, place one foot carefully on the ice, pausing long enough to settle yourself on the blade before following with your other foot.

Once on the ice, don't immediately try to move. Simply stand there, your hand lightly on the barrier, and get the "feel" of your blades and the slick surface underfoot. Stand erect and relaxed, with your feet parallel and comfortably apart, and your weight equally on both. Because you are unaccustomed to riding on two narrow strips of steel, your ankles will wobble and want to bend inward; keep them as still and as straight as you can. And, no doubt, you'll have to struggle a bit to maintain your balance. After a few moments, slide your skates back and forth to add to the overall feel of things.

Now try a few steps. While the gliding actions of skating are quite different from the heel-and-toe movements of walking, it is perfectly all right to walk and not skate these first few steps. Your whole purpose here is just to get some idea of what movement on your blades feels like. Keep your steps short, however, so that you won't slip, and the blades parallel to the ice so that you won't snag the toe picks.

If you wish to do so, you may go on gripping the barrier as you walk. But break free of it and move along on your own at the earliest possible moment. Balance comes with confidence and with getting the feel of the ice, and there can be no skating without it. You'll never get the hang of balance so long as you cling to some support.

After a few experimental "walks," come to a standstill again. Erect and relaxed, set your feet parallel to each other—about six inches apart—and settle your weight equally on both. Now bend your knees and ankles well forward, and let your pelvis ride directly forward over your feet. All the while, hold your back perfectly straight, keeping your head and shoulders erect.

Thus positioned, with your knees so deeply bent that you will be unable to see your feet should you glance down, you are in what is known as the basic *posture of skating.* It is the posture best assumed for all skating, for it enables you to carry out two vital functions. With it, you always move along on forward-bending knee and ankle, both of which contribute to your control and your look of grace. And with it, you always carry your weight solidly on your skates so that, as you shift from foot to foot, your center of gravity can be easily placed over the skate in use. Unless your center of gravity is over that skate, your balance will always be in jeopardy.

Now for a last experiment: Try another short walk, this time lifting each foot several inches off the ice so that you can stand for a moment on its companion. You will feel yourself automatically shift your weight to the skate in use; center your weight directly over it and keep your ankle firm and as straight as possible. Lift each foot straight up and then bring it straight down and close beside the other. This exercise will give you your first feel of balancing on one blade and of shifting your weight from skate to skate at just the right moment.

You've now been getting acquainted with the ice for several minutes. The time has come to begin actual skating—to try your first strokes. Here we go. . . .

Learning to Stroke

Stroking is the name given to the traditional skating action that propels you, either forward or backward, along the ice. The action, which is basic to every style of skating, consists of a series of individual strokes in which a thrust in a given direction is made with one blade and then followed by a glide for a time on the blade opposite, after which the feet exchange jobs for the next stroke.

You cannot learn to stroke properly by taking a deep breath, shoving off from the boards, and trying to thrust-and-glide your way across the ice in imitation of your fellow skaters. Stroking involves several details of balance and body placement, and so is best learned a step at a time. Before trying more than one stroke, you should learn how to push yourself forward from a standstill and how then to glide steadily on one skate for a few feet.

With the aid of the illustrations on the following pages, let's take a look at each action.

When you are ready to try your first forward thrust, stand erect and relaxed, with knees straight, feet parallel, and weight evenly distributed. Look straight ahead and extend your arms out from your sides, setting your hands, palms down, at about hip level. Make certain that your shoulders are level and, along with your hips, squared to the direction in which you will travel.

Still keeping your knees straight, place your feet in a T position by swinging your left foot smoothly in behind your right so that the instep of your left boot meets the heel of your right at a ninety-degree angle. Check to see that your movement has not altered the direction of your right skate; it should still be pointing straight along your intended line of travel. And check your shoulders and hips; be sure that they do not turn sideways (they may tend to do so) as you bring your left foot back. Now let your weight ride back onto your left foot.

At the same time, turn your left ankle deeply in so that the blade beneath tilts over on its inside edge and sets its full length against the ice. It is necessary that the inside edge be hard against the ice, for only then will it "bite" and propel you forward during

SKATES PARALLEL AT STANDSTILL

the coming thrust. If left flat, it will simply skid on the glassy surface.

Bend your knees deeply, allowing your right ankle to bend for-

SKATER IN T POSITION

ward along with your right knee. Now, for the thrust itself, straighten your left knee while holding your right knee bent. Your straightening leg will push the blade against the ice and set you in

SKATER WITH ANKLE BENT

motion. Push the *full length* of the blade against the ice; don't allow yourself to push with the toe picks, for the thrust will then be weak and clumsy. Remember, the picks are reserved for certain spins, jumps, and stops.

SKATER STRAIGHTENING LEG FOR THRUST

In the instant that you begin to move, bring your weight forward over your right skate. When your weight shifts, you must, as
skaters say, carry it forward "all in one piece." Try not to lead with
your shoulders or bend at the waist. Simply come forward

smoothly, with shoulders erect and back straight. Settle your weight directly and solidly on the skate so that your center of gravity is directly over it. Throughout, keep your right knee strongly bent. Imagine that your kneecap is an arrowhead pointing straight along your line of travel.

Once your left knee is fully straightened, allow your left skate to rise to a point between two and four inches off the ice. Bring it up naturally, at the same time turning your toes outward and slightly downward. Don't be tempted to try for an extra bit of

SKATER WITH ONE FOOT OFF ICE

thrust by flicking the picks against the ice. Again, the result will be a weak and clumsy thrust.

You are now gliding on one foot, and your job is to steer along as straight a line as possible. To do this, you need a steady ankle beneath you. Hold it bent forward along with your knee, but try to keep it from wobbling or dropping to one side or another. Straight-line skating requires that both blade edges be on the ice at the same time, and a wobbling or "dropped" ankle will veer you off course by tipping you onto one blade edge or the other. In time, you will come to use the edges deliberately so that you can describe skating's graceful curves and circles. But for now, just think about moving straight ahead and developing your balance and steadiness.

And above all, don't throw up your hands in disgust and head for home if your ankles insist on wobbling no matter how firmly you hold them. Everybody has to put up with their misbehavior when first skating. A few practice sessions will put the problem behind you for good.

You will help yourself keep to a straight line if you go on holding your hips and shoulders squared to your line of travel, just as they were when you pushed off. When they are squared to your line of travel, they are in what skaters call the *neutral position*, a term that we'll be much using from here on. But don't worry if they at first want to shift from side to side as you skate. It's what they do when you're walking, and it will take you a bit of time to break them of the habit.

When you have held the glide position for as long as possible, swing your left foot gently forward until it is directly alongside the right. You will need to straighten your right knee somewhat during this movement so that your left blade will remain clear of the ice as it travels. And you will need to keep the left blade parallel to the surface beneath. Otherwise, you run the risk of tripping yourself by snagging the toe picks.

Once the left skate is alongside the right, lower it slowly to the ice and glide for a time on two feet, again bending your knees, but just slightly this time.

There. You've managed your first forward thrust and glide. For the sake of illustration, the left foot was used for the pushoff, but you must now become equally adept at getting into motion on either foot. As often as possible in the next days, you should practice pushing off on one skate and then the other, concentrating always on straightening your thrusting leg smoothly, on keeping your hips and shoulders in the neutral position, on transferring

SKATER BRINGING LEFT FOOT FORWARD

your weight easily to your gliding blade, and on holding your forward knee bent and the ankle below firm as you glide.

Incidentally, we've talked about straightening one leg or the other at certain times during the beginning stroke. This same advice will be given repeatedly as you learn the various skating maneuvers. But you must always keep one point in mind. At all times, when one leg or the other is straight, it must *not* be so straight that the knee is stiff and locked in place. For the most graceful skating, always keep the knees slightly flexed.

As soon as you have the thrust and glide well in hand, it will be time to try a series of strokes. To do so, push off from the left foot and glide on the right. Then follow the illustrations below.

As you have already done, the skater pushed off on her left foot, and the photograph on page 34 shows her now in the exact moment when her feet have come together again at the close of the first stroke. With her, bend both knees deeply. Then . . .

. . . send your right leg out to the side, bending your ankle so that it presses the inside edge of the blade against the ice. As before, set the full length of the blade on the ice. And, as before, keep your forward knee bent in an arrowhead pointing straight along your line of travel.

Look closely at the skater on page 35, however, so that there will be no mistake about the difference between this new thrusting action and the original pushoff position. Since it is impossibly clumsy to return your foot to the T position of the pushoff, you must angle it off to the side. This "sideways" thrust must now be used for all subsequent strokes, whether made with the left or right foot.

All now goes as before. Your thrusting leg straightens to move you forward, and you send your weight out over your leading skate, in this instance, the left one. When your right leg is about fully straight, the skate below leaves the ice, holds for a moment behind you with toe pointed out and downward, and then swings forward until it is parallel with the left skate. As it touches the ice, you again bend your knees deeply and enter your next stroke by sending your left leg out to the side. For as long as you make your way around the rink, the stroking cycle repeats itself.

Once you've attempted your first stroking cycle, days of practice lie ahead, with your goal being a strong and graceful movement from foot to foot. As you practice, you will want to keep three pointers uppermost in mind:

SKATER IN TWO-FOOTED GLIDE BEFORE SECOND STROKE

First, as a beginner, you will take a longer time than is necessary gliding between strokes; work to shorten that time so that your next stroke begins in about the same instant that your feet come together at the close of the preceding stroke. Second, do not be

SKATER USING SIDEWAYS THRUST

reluctant to bend your knees deeply while gliding between strokes; you will be in a squatting position that at first seems ungainly and uncomfortable, but one that will become more comfortable as you reduce the gliding time between strokes. Finally, give special attention to shifting your weight from foot to foot as smoothly as possible; in the beginning, you may experience some difficulty in timing the start for each new stroke, but practice will soon take care of the problem.

CARE OF YOUR EQUIPMENT

Since you have managed a series of strokes during your first lesson, you can go home pretty proud of yourself, for some beginners require several sessions before reaching the stroking cycle. But you cannot call your first lesson complete without memorizing some additional pointers—pointers having to do with the care of your equipment.

It goes without saying that, with good care, even the most inexpensive equipment can give you good service. Poor care, however, will see the best of skates soon damaged and eventually ruined.

Here are five good-care tips that you should take away from the rink at the end of your first day and then remember for as long as you skate:

1. After use, wipe your boots and blades thoroughly with a dry cloth to remove all ice. Unattended moisture is your skate's worst enemy, pitting and rusting the blade, depriving the boot leather of its watertightness.

Skates should be wiped *immediately* after use. Never be in such a hurry to leave the rink that you delay the job until you arrive home. The moisture will be given too much of a chance to do harm. At home, store your skates in a dry place.

Various preparations—from creams to lacquers—can be bought for keeping your boots watertight. Some skaters think them unnecessary if the boots are routinely and thoroughly wiped. You will be wise to talk over the matter of preparations with your instructor or the rink manager. Either will be able to advise you on their use and on the best of their number.

Incidentally, regardless of whether you use an agent for keeping your boots watertight, you will be wise to coat the heels and soles now and again with an enamel made for that purpose. It will protect the heels and soles from rotting and will keep them from separating from each other.

2. Check your sole and heel plates periodically to see if use has loosened their screws. If so, tighten them immediately (you should carry a small screwdriver in your tote bag for this job). Once any screw has loosened itself, moisture quickly seeps in under the head and causes a rust that eventually damages the threads.

3. Keep an eye on your blades to see that they are always well sharpened. A dull blade, of course, will fail to grip the ice efficiently and will constantly tend to skid. As soon as your blades seem to be dulling, have them sharpened—*ground* is the word you'll hear around the rink. All rinks provide grinding services, usually for a small fee. It is a good idea to have your blades checked for sharpness after about every fifteen sessions on the ice.

4. At all times, resist the urge to sharpen your skates yourself. Neither try the job at home nor fiddle with the sharpening equipment at the rink. You can count on ruining your skates, for proper grinding, which consists of sharpening the edges and deepening the hollow, is a precise job requiring much experience. For instance, if improperly ground, the hollow may be cut too shallow or too deep; a too-shallow hollow causes a blade to skid, while a too-deep hollow permits the edges to sink into the ice more than is necessary, slowing all movement.

5. Last, always be sure to wear guards when you are not on the ice or on the rubber matting surrounding it. This precaution has already been mentioned, but it is of such importance that it bears repeating. Remember, any hard surface—from bare earth to concrete—can quickly damage the best of blades. Do not, however, leave the guards on when you store your skates at home. They will reduce air circulation and slow evaporation, giving excess moisture the chance to do harm.

FOUR

The Basics: Safety on Ice

As was said in the previous chapter, skating is anything but a dangerous sport. But it can be made so by just one thoughtless skater or "grandstander," perhaps the witless one who never watches where he is going, or perhaps the "ice bully" who can never pass another without cutting too close or jabbing with an elbow. He can be responsible for painful collisions and falls that not only mar another skater's enjoyment but that all too often result in injury.

Many newcomers are responsible for accidents not because they are thoughtless or rude, but simply because they have not yet learned the rules for safe skating. This chapter is being written so that you will know these rules and know best how to avoid injury to yourself or others.

Since you may be skating indoors or outdoors, we will talk of safety as it applies to the rink and to the neighborhood pond or stream. Additionally, we will describe the methods advised for quick and efficient rescue in the event of that common and most feared outdoor skating accident: the crash through thin ice.

Let's look first at safety on rink ice. You will skate without being a threat to yourself or those around you if you will keep just ten points in mind:

Safety Indoors

1. If you own speed skates, they are best left at home. Intended for racing, they can tempt you to speeds that are obviously unsafe in traffic that is usually moving at a slower pace. Too, their long blades pose a constant threat to the surrounding skaters; all too easily, they can stab the leg of a passerby or trip him up. Many rinks prohibit the use of speed blades for general skating. The blades should be worn only when you are working out alone or with other speed skaters.

2. Skaters travel in one direction—usually counterclockwise—when on rink ice. Always move in that same direction. Never "grandstand" by skating against traffic. And never swing about and thread your way back through oncoming traffic to reach a friend, even if he is only several feet away. Wrong-way skating is one of the chief causes of rink collisions.

3. Whenever you come onto the ice, pick an open spot in traffic, skate parallel to the barrier for a few yards, and gradually ease your way out to a travel lane. Do not charge onto the ice and sail across the line of other skaters. And never enter the ice without checking the oncoming traffic.

4. Do nothing to hinder your fellow skaters. Stay as well away from them as traffic conditions permit. Resist all temptations to brush against a friend, give him a playful push, or cut too sharply in front of him—all can end in a collision or can cause your victim to fall. In particular, never try to tease or otherwise disturb a friend who is just learning to skate. His balance, as you know from your own beginning experience, is too delicate for comfort.

5. At all times, watch where you're going. While a beginner must keep an eye out for fellow skaters, you are even more responsible to watch out for him as you grow more experienced. Remember, he can stumble, fall, or skitter into your path at any time. Your swift reaction and agility can avoid an accident—but only if you're on the alert so that you can see the coming trouble in time.

6. Many rinks set aside special periods for expert, speed, beginning, or couples skating during a session. Such periods usually last a

few moments each and, if you are not going to skate accordingly, remain clear of the ice until ordinary skating resumes. Nothing annoys experts more than the novice who comes struggling along when he should be out at the refreshment stand. Likewise, nothing frustrates newcomers more than the so-called "flash" who insists on cavorting in their midst.

7. Traditionally, the center of the ice is left open to skaters who wish to practice certain maneuvers, figures, or dance steps. Leave them in peace and do not distract them by attempting general skating there. And don't stand on the inside edge of the traffic flow to watch anyone at practice. If you're going to be a spectator for even a few moments, get completely off the ice.

8. Whenever you fall, rise as quickly as you can, leave the ice, or continue skating. Do not sit or sprawl for any time while you laugh or show your disgust, for you then constitute a formidable barrier for the skaters approaching from behind. Hopefully, they will be able to take evasive action, but don't put them to the test. Clear a path for them by returning to your feet immediately.

Above all, don't "dramatize" your fall by lying there and pretending that you are hurt. Silly as it is, this trick is attempted by more newcomers than you would at first think, usually as a way of covering their embarrassment, but sometimes because they imagine that they are actually hurt. It sends your fellow skaters and the rink personnel rushing to your aid, causes a traffic jam, and, of course, irritates all concerned when you're found to be "faking."

9. Learn the correct way to fall and then to rise again. Let your key word be *relax* when you feel your skates go out from under you. While yet a learner, you will automatically stiffen and begin to swing your arms in an effort to maintain your balance, but these actions are apt to send you over on your back with a thud heard clear out to the rink shop. So tell yourself to go limp, and then bend your knees and literally sink to the ice. It is a knack that you will soon develop, particularly when you find that most ice falls are not as bad as those on floors or the ground. When you fall while moving, you slide along the ice and thereby reduce the direct impact.

SKATERS DEMONSTRATING RIGHT AND WRONG METHODS OF
RISING AFTER A FALL

To rise efficiently, you need imitate the skater on the left in the illustration. Roll over on one hip, come up on one knee with your hands on the ice, bring the opposite skate under you, and then thrust yourself to a standing position. Never try to rise in the manner being attempted by the skater on the right. Without fail, your skates will slide out from under you, and you'll end up sitting on the ice again.

10. The subject of falls brings us to our last pointer: Always doublecheck to see that you have removed your skate guards before venturing out from the sidelines. If you accidentally wear them onto the ice, you can be guaranteed that your feet will immediately go out from under you and that you will sit down with a clatter and a thump that will turn every eye in the rink toward you. Talk about a bruised ego! This is the time for it. Thanks to your forgetfulness, you'll feel like the greenest of greenhorns.

But take heart. At one time or another, every skater overlooks his guards and sails out onto the ice for an immediate crash landing. It happens even to the best of professionals.

Once you've fallen, don't try to stand again on the guards and beat a hasty retreat to the sidelines. You will never make it. Down you'll go—time and again. You have no choice but to sit where you are and remove the guards, with your seat getting wetter and colder by the second. In the long run, however, a damp rear will prove better than an endless array of tumbles on your way back to safety.

Safety Out-of-Doors

A frozen pond or stream, obviously, poses a number of hazards not to be found in an indoor rink. Indoors, you never need be concerned with the solidity of the ice underfoot. Indoors, you can usually skate safely alone, certain that help is close by in the event of a serious fall. Indoors, you can be sure that you are surrounded only by skaters, all of them engaged in the same activity as you.

Not so on a frozen pond or stream. Here, you have to contend with ice of varying thicknesses. Here, you must always skate with companions close by so that you will have immediate help available in case of a crash through weak or broken ice. Here, you must always keep in mind what you must do should you or a friend suffer a breakthrough. And here, you must skate in the midst of various other winter activities—from iceboating and ice fishing to informal hockey games—making certain that you remain prudently clear of them.

Outdoor ice skating is unquestionably one of the most enjoyable and exhilarating of sports. The air is sharp and cold against your face, and deep in your lungs. Your skin tingles and glows. The winter-cloaked scenery dazzles the eye. But all the joy ends abruptly in the moment of accident. Most outdoor accidents, however, can be avoided with the following common-sense rules. In all, they number five:

1. Before ever gliding out onto a frozen pond or stream, take a few moments to check your surroundings. First, determine the

thickness of the ice to assure yourself that it can support you. If it is an inch or less thick, stay away from it, for it is unsafe for even the most lightweight skater. In general, a two-inch thickness is needed to carry one person, while three inches can usually accommodate as many as four or five skaters. Four-inch ice is customarily strong enough for all skating and most other winter activities.

Take an extra look at the ice close to the shore. The pond may be supporting a dozen skaters out there at its center, but don't plunge off the shore at any random spot. Since the ice there is customarily much thinner than farther out, do as the skaters before you have done. Select a spot thick enough to carry you before you enter the ice.

Do not limit your safety check to thickness alone. Take special care if the ice is "old," particularly if spring is at hand and the ice has been around all winter long. Even when eight or more inches thick, old ice can be honeycombed with cracks and breaks. And look to the color of the surface. With "black ice," you can be well assured that you're on a solid surface. But not so with "white ice" or salt-water ice; both are always considered hazardous.

If you are skating after a fresh snowfall, brush the snow away from in front of you as you move out from the shore. Check for hidden cracks, weak spots, and even broken and open areas. And, if the spring thaw is under way, test the solidity very closely. A thaw can alter the makeup of ice in a matter of hours.

Finally, take a look at the off-ice facilities. Think twice about skating if there is not at hand (a) a guard trained in ice rescue, (b) rescue and first-aid equipment, (c) an emergency telephone, and (d) accommodations for warming and caring for yourself after a fall through the ice. You will usually find facilities such as these, plus refreshment stands and dressing areas, at outdoor skating spots that are maintained for public use. Too, public "outdoor rinks" routinely check the ice and mark off danger spots with posted warnings. You need to be doubly certain of your rescue abilities and those of your companions if you choose an isolated or untended stretch of ice.

2. Once you are on the ice, apply the same courtesies and safety

precautions required at an indoor rink. Give others ample room for skating. Skate in the direction that traffic is moving. Resist all temptations at horseplay. Be particularly thoughtful of beginners.

Pond or stream areas maintained for the public ordinarily reserve special areas for various activities—one spot for skating, another for games, another for iceboating, and so on. Remain in the area reserved for skating.

3. Should your "outdoor" rink be an unsupervised pond, stream, or other body of water, never venture out on it by yourself. Always have friends nearby to lend a hand should there be an emergency. Even if you feel thoroughly experienced in the techniques of self-rescue, avoid skating alone. Remember, in the event of an accident, you may not be in any condition to help yourself.

Even when skating in an area maintained for the public, do not drift too far away from the other skaters. Should you run into trouble, they may not hear your cries or may be unable to reach you in time to be of real assistance.

4. All the while that you are skating, keep your eye out for weak or broken spots in the ice. In either supervised or unsupervised areas, warn your fellow skaters of any danger spots sighted. If possible, post the area with a warning sign in an unsupervised area. In a supervised area, hunt up the area manager so that he can post a warning immediately.

5. Avoid skating at dusk or at night unless the area permits it and provides ample lighting.

Now let's look at the all-important rules of ice rescue, at first answering the question: "How can I save myself?"

SAVING YOURSELF

Let's say that, even while keeping an eye out for danger spots, you accidentally skate onto a section of weak ice. You hear an ominous cracking sound directly underfoot. Before you have the chance to glide to safety, the surface gives way. You plunge feet first into icy water.

1. Your first rule is: *Don't panic.* The cold water, the sudden-

ness of your fall, and the knowledge that you're in trouble will drive the breath out of you and cause your heart to hammer. But don't lose your head. Don't waste your energy by thrashing your arms wildly and gulping in water as you cry for help. Save your cries for a moment or so.

2. As you fall, spread your arms wide so that they may catch the sides of the break and keep you from going under the water. You may not think that you will have time for this, but you'll be surprised how fast your arms will move once you give them the order. This is one more reason for keeping your head—for only then will you have the wit to give your arms the proper command in time for it to be of benefit.

If your arms catch the sides of the break, they will keep you from going under the water and perhaps slipping under the solid ice around the break. Holding the sides of the break, begin to kick your feet in a flutter kick. This will help to keep them from jackknifing under the ice and carrying you down under with them.

Should you find yourself beneath the ice, do not blindly try to kick and thrash your way back to the opening. Open your eyes so that you can see where you are going. Look around to find where light is reflecting on the water in the break. Then make your way to it.

3. Once you've fallen through, do not immediately try to climb back out. Take a moment to check the edges of the break. They may prove too weak to support your weight as you attempt to climb out and so will only give way beneath you, plunging you back into the water and eating away at your energy. Climb out only when the ice seems strong enough to support you.

In the meantime, break your way through the thin ice until you come to a solid area. Now propel your body up onto the ice with a strong kick and a lunge forward. When you feel your hips come clear of the water, stretch your arms beyond your head and then roll out and away from the hole. Keep rolling and then crawling until you are safely away from the break.

Why the roll? It will distribute your weight over a wider area of ice and so protect you from further cave-in. Were you to stand up, the ice might not yet be strong enough to support your weight concentration.

And why the outstretched arms? They will increase your leverage on the ice and enable you to roll away from the hole more swiftly.

If you wish, you may be able to give yourself a couple of firm "handrails" to assist your climb back to safety. You can pull off your mittens, place them on the ice alongside the break, and give them a moment to freeze, after which you can use them as grips to support yourself as you inch forward and onto the surface. You should, however, save this strategy until you have tried to climb out by the earlier-mentioned conventional method. It takes time for the mittens to freeze and, all the while, the icy water is biting deeper into your clothes—and into you.

4. Once you are back to safety, don't stand around and pour the story of your adventure out to your friends. You won't feel like talking for a time anyway, and so roll yourself in the snow to absorb the water from your clothing. Warm and dry yourself and get into dry clothes as soon as possible.

Rescuing a Friend

If a fellow skater falls through the ice, take action immediately. You're bound to stand there in frozen shock for a moment, but cut that moment to a minimum. Don't delay to see if he is able to get out by himself. If rescue equipment is nearby, run for it, making sure that you mark the location of the accident in your mind so that you will be able to go directly to it on your way back. Or you might leave a coat, a glove, or some other handy object behind as a marker. Then:

1. Bring up a pole, a ladder, a rope, even a tree branch or a sled —anything that can be stretched across the thin ice to the hole. When you come near the hole, lie down before sending the rescue gear across to him; the ice underfoot, though hopefully not as thin as at the breakthrough point, may be too weak to take the weight concentration of standing. As soon as your friend grabs the rescue gear, pull it slowly toward you to assist him as he climbs out. Once out, he should roll quickly away from the hole. If it is not safe for

him to do so, keep pulling the gear slowly forward until he is again on a solid surface. If he rolls to safety, don't stand up to congratulate him; back away on your stomach until you are certain that *you* are again on perfectly solid ice.

2. Should you be alone and without rescue gear and have to move closer to the opening, again get down on your stomach and inch forward. Come only as close as needs be and then extend a belt, a scarf, a coat—anything at hand—to the victim, after which you pull back slowly to help him clear of the break.

3. If you are without equipment but have companions with you, form a human chain, with all of you down on your stomachs, each man gripping the ankles of the person in front of him. Let the lightest person in the group be the link closest to the break. Once he has gripped the victim's wrist or thrown something such as a belt to him, move the chain slowly back and away from the break. Do not break the chain and stand up until all links and the accident victim are on solid ice.

4. Most public outdoor skating areas are equipped with rescue ropes, some of which have buoys attached. Should you use a rope instead of a pole—or in conjunction with it—never simply hold one end in your hands, for, if they are cold and numb, it can all too easily be dropped. Too, you may need your hands free for other jobs. Tie the rope around your waist before tossing the opposite end to the rescue victim. Of the kinds of rescue ropes available, the type with a buoy attached can prove especially useful. Should the person being rescued fall back into the water as he is attempting his escape, he can use the buoy for extra support.

5. Once the victim has reached safety, treat him as you would yourself. Have him roll in the snow to absorb the water from his clothes. Get him dried and warm and into fresh clothes as soon as possible.

To many a skater, it is far more fun to glide along an outdoor surface, with the winter scenery all about, than to circle an enclosed rink. And, indeed, it is. But a price must be paid for all the beauty. That price is double attention to the rules of ice safety. By not observing them, there is always danger. By observing them, there is nothing in store but pleasure.

FIVE

The Basics: Adding to Your First Skills

When first on the ice, you will have your hands full just keeping your balance and trying to skate in a straight line. But what happens when you finally have to stop, or need to curve back in the opposite direction at the end of the rink? For the stop, you'll probably hope for the best and use the time-honored methods of either deliberately falling down or sailing into the barrier with hands outstretched. As for the curve, no doubt you'll plant both feet gingerly on the ice and then trace a wavering path sideways by forcing your toes over in the direction you want to travel.

None of these methods—though they will get the job done for you—is much to brag about and so, even while you are working on your stroking cycle, you should begin to try your first stops and curves. Then take a deep breath, for you'll next need to learn how to skate backward and how to turn yourself from front to back while in motion.

These four skills are to be the subjects of this chapter and the next. To begin, let's see what it's like to apply your "ice brakes."

PUTTING ON YOUR BRAKES

In all, there are five basic methods for coming to a stop while skating. Two of their number are meant for use while skating backward, and so they will have to be held for the next chapter. Remaining are the *snowplow*, the *T stop*, and the *hockey stop*.

We'll talk about all three here, but you should know that the T and hockey stops call for more skill than you have at this moment. You should save them for the time, soon to come, when you feel a bit more confident on your blades. You can, however, give the snowplow a try on your first day at the rink—and the odds are that you will master it before you head for home.

The Snowplow

The snowplow is strictly a beginner's stop and is intended for use only during your initial days of skating. Easy to learn, it will

SNOWPLOW STOP

save you the embarrassment of crashing into the barrier, but, since it is the trademark of the novice, you should put it aside as soon as you have gained enough proficiency to experiment with one of the other stops.

When you are ready to try your first snowplow, end your stroking actions and bring your feet parallel to each other, but about eighteen inches apart. Then, without closing the distance between your feet, bend your knees somewhat deeply, lean back a bit, and turn your toes inward. Simultaneously, drop your ankles slightly so that your inside edges bit into the ice and serve as your brakes. You will slowly skid to a stop—and that's all there is to it.

Just two pointers, however: The amount of ankle bend is vital to the stop. If you fail to bend your ankles at all, your blades will skid helplessly on the ice, but if you give them too much bend, the edges will bite too deeply for an easy skid. Above all, do not allow them to bend outward so that you are riding on your outside edges. Your blades will then run in toward each other and likely send you stumbling or to your hands and knees.

The T Stop

The T stop is a favorite of both general and figure skaters. It is a braking action that is both graceful and efficient. You will find that it can be mastered with relative ease once you have gained confidence in your balance and stroking cycle.

The stop gets its name from the T position into which the feet are placed. It may be executed with either the left or the right foot to your rear, but for the sake of illustration, let's try it with the right foot. It should then be practiced on one foot and then the other until each can handle it with equal ease.

Ready? End your stroking cycle and glide for a moment with both feet close together. Next, keeping your blade parallel to the ice, swing your right foot in behind the left and place it just off the ice so that it slants behind the left in a rough approximation of the T position. Now lower the skate to the ice and then lean back, put your weight on the skate, and press the blade onto its outside edge. With the edge serving as a brake, you will skid gently to a stop.

In executing the stop for the first time, you should work slowly and deliberately, pausing for a moment before lowering your right foot to the ice after it assumes the T position. This will give you the "feel" of the position, but, of course, you will need to eliminate

T Stop

the pause as you go on. In time, the stop should become one continuous and flowing movement.

Two pointers: Always lean firmly back so that you go onto the outside edge of your braking blade. Avoid the inside edge, for the blade will then drag on the ice, pull your body sideways, and veer you off course. Be sure, too, that your braking blade is held parallel to the ice as you swing it back and into the T position. If you allow your toes to angle iceward, the picks will likely scrape against the surface. You'll come to a stop, all right—but you'll do so by stumbling or falling.

The Hockey Stop

The fastest stop of all is the hockey stop and, as its name indicates, it is often used in the high-speed game of hockey. No matter how fast you are traveling, it will tug you to a halt in short order amidst a shower of flying ice. As a general or figure skater, you will likely depend more on the T stop for your braking actions, but it is well to learn the hockey stop so that it can be used in cases of emergency.

The stop is a simple one to describe. Bring your feet parallel to each other and about a blade's length apart. Then, holding your arms, shoulders, and head in the neutral position, turn both heels sharply to your right. Bring them solidly around until they are at right angles to your line of travel. At the same time, lean far back and bend your knees deeply. You will skid quickly to a stop on the inside edge of your right skate and the outside edge of your left. You may also perform the stop by swinging your heels to the left, in which case your braking edges will be reversed.

When you first see the stop performed and watch the shower of ice that rises from under the blades, you may feel a bit uneasy about trying it yourself. But, though it does require some skill, experienced skaters will tell you that it is not as difficult to execute as it may look. If you will try it first at slow speeds, all will be well. One common error, however, must be avoided, for it can result in a nasty spill.

Always keep your feet parallel as you swing your heels. Often,

THE HOCKEY STOP

a skater will allow one skate (his right one if he is swinging right) to slide out in front of the other. Were his feet parallel, each blade would skid right along its own line of travel and bring him to a stop. But, with one foot passing ahead of the other, he puts himself into a spin that throws him off balance. The same kind of spin, incidentally, is created when you allow your shoulders to turn with your heels. Keep them always squared to your line of travel.

Another pointer: When first attempting the stop, you may find that, instead of coming to the expected halt, you simply go gliding off at an angle. Two factors, either singly or in combination, are responsible. You've failed to swing your heels around far enough, or you've turned them too slowly. In either case, the blade edges have been unable to bite the ice. Always bring your heels around to full right angles—and always bring them around smartly.

CURVES AND CROSSOVERS

When you come to the end of the rink for the first time and need to curve around in the opposite direction, there is no need for you to stop or sail into the barrier. If you can steer a bicycle, you can get around that curve with no trouble at all.

All you need do is end your stroking action and glide on two feet. During the glide, simply turn your arms as if you are aiming your bike into the curve. You'll feel yourself start to swing in the desired direction.

After that, go on "steering the bike" until you leave the curve at the opposite side of the rink.

This simple maneuver will not only carry you through the adventure of your first curves, but also will give you the beginning "feel" of deliberately skating on your edges. As you grow more experienced, you will be using them more and more, for, as said earlier, they make possible all the curves and changes of direction that are the hallmarks of figure skating. For now, the movement of your arms will shift your weight so that you go naturally over on the edges, just enough over on them to send you along an arcing path.

Once you have glided through a number of curves in this fashion, you may wish to try an exercise that will give you a stronger idea of what it is like to skate on your edges. Imitating the skater in the photograph, glide forward with your feet together for a time and then do no more than lean in the direction in which you wish to travel.

But imitate the skater exactly. As she is doing, lean "all in one piece," establishing a straight line right up from your blade edges

TWO-FOOTED GLIDE

to the top of your head; avoid the temptation to hold your ankles erect and lean the rest of you above them. And keep your feet close together throughout; do not permit the outside leg (your right leg on a left curve) to drift off to the side as if trying to stroke. Interfering with the exercise, both are errors usually committed in the hope of steadying your balance. Both are unnecessary for balance and will send you along a too-straight path by angling your body up and away from the line of the curve.

Of course, the "bicycle" strategy and two-footed glide are meant only for your first days on the ice. As soon as you are able, you will want to stroke your way through the curves at the end of the rink. To do so, you will need the *forward crossover*.

The forward crossover may be executed while curving left or right. Often called a *run*, it will increase your speed on the curve, a fact that makes it a favorite of racing skaters. If you are right-handed, you will likely find it easier to perform on a left curve, but you should strive to become quite as adept in the opposite direction as well.

When ready to try your first forward crossover to the left, stand in the T position with your left foot ahead. This time, however, do not hold your shoulders in the neutral position, but bring your right arm and shoulder forward while letting your left arm and shoulder ride back. Now bend your knees deeply and push off as if entering the ordinary stroking cycle. Carry your weight forward so that you are riding on the outside edge of the left skate and thus moving on a curve.

Once your thrusting right skate, with toe pointed out and down, comes off the ice, swing it forward as you would in a regular stroke. But now carry it past your left skate and, as pictured, cross it wide in front of your left leg and lower it so that it touches the ice with its inside edge. Your ankles will now be crossed, and your feet should be exactly parallel to each other.

Instantly, shift your weight to your right leg and bend its knee deeply. Now your left leg should straighten, thrust, and then rise easily out behind and across the right. Your left skate should come off the ice with toe pointed and, in that moment, you should be an exact copy of the skater pictured on page 58. Hold the position for a little time and then . . .

. . . swing your left skate forward and lower it to the ice along-side the right. Then stroke forward by thrusting the right skate off to the side and, again, repeat the crossover movement. For as long as you continue through the curve with the crossover, you will need to repeat the sequence: stroke, crossing movement, stroke.

As you now practice the crossover, you will need to keep three

Ankles Crossed in Crossover

LEFT LEG EXTENDED IN CROSSOVER

pointers uppermost in mind: First, imagine that you are skating in a circle (as indeed you are, for every curve in skating, if continued long enough, will end in a circle), and then always lean well toward the center of that circle—and always at the same angle. An inadequate lean or a wavering lean will invariably produce an awkward, indecisive crossover.

Second, your forward knee—at first the left and then the right—must be deeply bent at all times. Work to bend it always to the same degree. If you vary the bend, you will look as if you are "bobbing" through the crossover.

Finally, always carry your left leg back and *across* your right in the action that follows the crossing of the ankles. A common beginning mistake is to allow the left leg to ride straight back. This will weaken your crossover action and may cause you to run in a straight line rather than along a curving one.

When you can execute a crossover to the left smoothly, it will be time to experiment in the opposite direction. Here, all will be reversed, but you will still need to keep the above three pointers in mind. And, as said at the beginning of this section, you may expect to find this new crossover a bit more difficult to master. Practice, however, should soon take care of the problem.

Now take that deep breath that we mentioned back at the start of the chapter. It's time to learn how to skate backward.

SIX

The Basics: Skating Backward

All instructors say that you should learn to skate backward as soon as possible, even while yet trying to get the knack of stroking forward. Their reasoning: the prospect of sailing backward across the ice often unnerves the beginner. He usually feels certain that he will lose his balance or crash blindly into another skater. And so the sooner he attempts his first backward strokes, the sooner he will get over his misgivings. But the longer he waits, the greater they may grow.

Granted, if you're not with an instructor or not in an area reserved for learning, the possibility of collision on a crowded rink may make your first efforts difficult. But a friend can always serve as lookout. Or you may be able to use the practice area at the center of the ice. As for keeping your balance, you can start with the simplest method known for skating backward: sculling.

Using the photographs as guides, let's give it a first try.

To begin, stand in imitation of the skater above left, with head and shoulders squared to your line of travel and with arms extended and hands at hip level. Keeping your weight equally distributed between both feet, bend your knees inward, and point the tips of your skates toward each other.

Next, with the skater above right, move your feet apart, forcing

TWO SKATERS IN BEGINNING SCULLING ACTIONS

TWO SKATERS IN FINAL SCULLING ACTIONS

them to ride away from each other on their inside edges. You will set up a thrust that will move you backward. Your arms will rise automatically to maintain your balance and help your movement.

When your feet are well apart (let them ride out as far as comfort will permit), straighten your knees and draw your skates together again with the skater below left. Throughout, keep your head and shoulders squared to your line of travel. Remain on your inside edges. Your arms will drop slightly as your feet approach each other.

At the end of the movement, as demonstrated by the skater below right, your feet should be together again, the heels almost touching. Do not pause at this point, but immediately bend your knees, aim the toes of your boots at each other once more, and slide your feet out to the sides again. Continually repeat the process for as long as you are on the move. With a little practice, you should be able to scull across the ice in a series of flowing, nonstop actions.

Now for an actual backward stroke. Begin to scull along the ice, but, when you come to the end of your second or third cycle and are gliding backward with feet together, bend both knees deeply. Then, imitating the skater pictured, transfer your weight to your right skate and, in the very same instant, send your left skate sliding out in front of you and bring it a few inches off the ice. Straighten your right knee as you do so.

Be sure to straighten your left knee as the skate leaves the ice and then point your toes to give an added look of grace to the movement. After the skate has been held suspended for a moment, swing it back until it is close alongside your right foot and exactly parallel to it, but do not lower it to the ice just yet. Now bend your right knee and turn the heel of your right skate outward to about a forty-five-degree angle, just as if it were executing a sculling action by itself. Allow the skate to go over on its inside edge as it moves. And, to propel yourself along, push it against the ice by straightening your right knee. You will look like the skater pictured.

At this point drop your left skate to the ice, immediately switch your weight to it, and bend the knee above strongly.

Left Skate off the Ice in Backward Stroke

The shift of your weight will enable you now to slide the right skate out to your front and up from the ice. Straighten your right knee as the skate comes up and point your toe, just as before. Then, as before, swing the skate back alongside its companion without

WEIGHT SHIFT TO LEFT LEG IN BACKWARD SKATING ACTION

touching the ice, turn your left heel out to a forty-five-degree angle, and thrust yourself along by straightening the knee above. Finally, drop your right skate to the ice and shift your weight to it. You will have completed a full stroking cycle and will be ready for another.

SKATERS BEGINNING TURN

One pointer: Whenever you extend one leg or the other to the front, you will find that it comes off the ice slightly to the side. To give yourself a thoroughly graceful look, you should not only point your toes but should gently swing the skate over until it is in a direct line with the leg on which you are riding.

Once you have learned to move backward along the ice, the way will be open to much varied action in your skating. In addition to the skills already learned, you can now begin to add turns, backward stops, and back crossovers.

A Simple Turn

The terms *curves* and *turns* often confuse the beginner. In everyday life, they usually mean much the same thing, for many a turn involves a curving action, while there is always a turning action when a curve is executed. But in skating they have quite distinct meanings.

SKATERS COMPLETING TURN

As you know, a curve is an arcing movement that, if continued for a long enough time, will end in a circle. But when you perform a turn on the ice, you switch from skating forward to skating backward (or vice versa) without changing the direction of your travel.

For our first experiments with the turn, we'll stick to a very simple one. Later we'll try the more complex and graceful *three-turn* and *mohawk* actions. But for the present, all that is needed is an easy movement that will give you the "feel" of swinging from forward to backward skating while in motion. Here it is now:

With the skater on the left on page 65, glide for a time on two feet, keeping your head and shoulders in the neutral position, and your feet parallel and about six inches apart. When you are ready to turn, join the skater on the right on page 65 in moving your left blade forward without lifting it from the ice. Simultaneously, shift most of your weight to your right foot.

Now, as the skater on the left on this page is doing, turn your left foot out and position it so that the heels of your skates are angling toward each other and still about six inches apart. Continue to hold most of your weight on your right skate. This position will set you moving into the turn.

Hold the position until the turn is about halfway completed. Then, with the skater on the right on page 66, swing your right blade around so that it is running parallel with the left. You will now be moving backward along your original line of travel. To complete all action, slide your right skate back until your feet are together and glide for a little time, after which you can begin a backward stroking cycle.

One pointer: When you shift your weight to your right foot, concentrate on keeping the blade running in as straight a line as possible. You may have a tendency to drop onto your inside edge and cause the blade to run to the left and across your line of travel. If it is permitted to do so, you will likely brake to a stop instead of continuing into the turn.

By itself, this simple turn, which can be made either to the right or the left, will add much zest to your skating. Additionally, it will serve as a fine introduction to the more exciting turns that we'll try in the next chapter.

Backward Stopping

The basic ways to stop while skating backward are two: the *back toe scratch* and the *back T stop*. The former is quite simple and can be learned in minutes. The latter is preferred by experienced skaters because of its graceful look.

The Back Toe Scratch

All you need do to perform the back toe scratch is, first, bring your feet close together and then slide your left skate out behind you for about a blade's length. Next, while leaning forward, slowly lift the heel of the left skate until the toe picks scrape the ice and brake you to a stop. Throughout, your braking leg should be straight, and your forward knee bent.

And that's all there is to it. The stop can be performed with either leg serving as the brake. Along with the snowplow, it is principally of value to beginners, enabling them to halt without sailing into the barrier or deliberately falling down. As soon as you are able, you will want to try the more graceful back T stop.

BACK TOE SCRATCH

The Back T Stop

In common with the forward T stop, this braking action can be made with either the right or the left foot. In time, you should be

BACK T STOP

able to use each foot with equal ease, but for now let's give it a try with the right skate, just as we did when experimenting with the forward version.

With head and shoulders in the neutral position, skate backward for a short distance. Then, at a time when your feet are parallel, lift your right skate and swing it in close behind the left, setting it at right angles and holding it clear of the ice with bended knee. Once in the T position, let your weight ride forward over your left skate and bend the knee deeply. At the same time, extend your right leg back a few inches, straightening its knee as you do, and finally lower your blade to the ice so that it skids along lightly on its inside edge and brings you to a stop.

One pointer: The secret of the successful back T stop is to know just the right amount of pressure to put on the braking skate. Too much pressure will cause the blade to bite hard and bring you to a clumsy, sometimes skittering stop. You'll need to experiment a bit before you find the exact amount needed.

BACK CROSSOVERS

The back crossover is a rough approximation of the forward crossover. With it, you may curve to the right or the left at great speed. Let's first try a left—or counterclockwise—curve. As usual, we'll follow the skaters in the illustrations.

With your right arm and shoulder back, and your left arm and shoulder forward, skate backward for a time. Then join the skater on the left above in gliding in a curve with your left foot slightly forward and your weight on the outside edge of your right skate. Now, as the skater on the right above is doing, execute a semicircular thrust with your left foot to move yourself along. Your skate will first slide away from the path of the curve, but should then return to it and pass across in front of your right skate.

Do not lift your left blade from the ice at any time during the thrust and the passage across the front of your right foot. Once the left skate has traveled as far as it will go, your ankles will be crossed, as are those of the skater on the left below. Now, with the skater on the right below, shift your weight to the left skate. Im-

SKATERS IN FIRST BACK CROSSOVER ACTIONS

SKATERS IN NEXT BACK CROSSOVER ACTIONS

Skater in Final Back Crossover Action

mediately, bring your right blade gently up from the ice and carry it around behind the heel of the left skate until you can place it on the ice well to the inside of the curve and with its blade tip on a level with the back of the left heel. With this move, the back crossover sequence is completed and you are in a position to repeat it. And repeat it you should—for as long as need be. Throughout any sequence, the thrusting left skate should *never* leave the ice.

Now for the right curve: Again skate backward and then glide for a moment, this time on the outside edge of your left skate, and with your right skate extended to your front. Using the semicircular thrust, swing your right leg across in front of your left without bringing it up from the ice. Once your ankles are safely crossed, transfer your weight to your right blade, lift your left skate from the ice, and pass it behind your heel until it can be returned to the surface well inside the line of the curve. Repeat the sequence throughout the curve, never raising the thrusting right skate from the ice.

Some pointers: As with the forward crossover, keep the upper part of your body firmly turned toward the center of the imaginary circle being skated, doing so by pressing the appropriate arm and shoulder forward while holding the opposite arm and shoulder back. At all times, make certain that your knees are bent when you transfer your weight from one skate to the other. This will add grace to the movement by avoiding a look of bobbing. Finally, to help yourself hold to a steady curve, always keep your eyes on the center of the imaginary circle.

In just two chapters, we've experimented with a wide variety of beginning movements—all the way from the first forward stroking cycle to back crossovers. But just because we have called them beginning or basic actions, do not make the mistake of thinking that they must all be attempted in your first session. Each must be practiced so that you will be as steady and as confident as possible on your blades before trying another. Many a young person has abandoned skating out of discouragement because he has hurried too much and has tried new movements before being ready for them. So take your time. Spend as many sessions as are needed to develop one movement to the point where you can easily advance to the next.

Your patience will pay dividends. In time it will bring you to expert status.

SEVEN

The Basics: The Art of Curving

Long before you've finished practicing the material in this chapter and the next, you'll likely be thinking of yourself as a sort of "Leaning Tower of Pisa" on ice. For you're going to spend all your time over on your blade edges, learning how to execute three curving movements: first the basic *edge*, then the *turn* on the curve, and finally the *roll*. All are exciting to perform; and all are vital to your skating future, for, once mastered, they will make you the "complete pleasure skater" and open the way to the challenge and fun of actual figure work.

Before gliding out on the ice to try your first edge, though, you should take time to add a few new terms to your skating vocabulary. Otherwise you may be in for some confusing moments.

New Words for Your Skating Vocabulary

Skaters have long given two meanings to the term *edges*. The first, of course, refers to the actual edges on the blades. But since you must always lean to the side and ride on your blade edges if you hope to travel along a curving path, the word has also come to mean the curve itself. This second meaning probably began to take shape when early skaters found that each blade edge cuts a tracing of the curve into the ice. It is easy to imagine them pointing at a curving line and saying, "There's the edge."

The edges to be learned in this chapter are curves that swing back to their starting points to form one or a series of full circles. They are skated on one foot only—either the right or the left—and may be performed while you are moving forward or backward. In all, there are four basic edges, with each named for the blade edge being used and the direction of your travel. They are: the *inside forward edge*, the *outside forward edge*, the *inside backward edge*, and the *outside backward edge*.

Thanks to the fact that you have two feet, however, each name actually covers two ways in which its edge can be skated. For instance, you can glide through the inside forward edge by using the inside edge of either your right or your left blade. If skated on the right blade, the curve is known as a "right inside forward edge." On the opposite skate, it becomes a "left inside forward edge." Consequently, to your skating vocabulary, you need now add a whole series of new names: "right" and "left" outside forward edges, "right" and "left" inside backward edges, and so forth.

Each is a mouthful to say, and so skaters have made things easier for themselves by abbreviating the various names. First, they long ago dropped from each name the term *edge*; today, you'll most often hear the curves telegraphically designated as, say, "right inside forwards" or "left outside forwards"; just as long ago, the word *backward* was cut to *back*, turning the backward curves into such as "right outside backs" and "left inside backs."

Additionally, when writing, a skater saves time by penciling just the initials of the blade edge he will use and the direction in which he will face while skating a curve. When mapping out a series of planned curves in a skating routine, he will never write that he intends to skate at one time or another on his Right Outside or his Left Inside blade edge while traveling Forward. Rather, he will simply jot down RFO or RFI.

To save space—and to acquaint you with these letter abbreviations so that you will be able to use them with ease at the rink— your blade edges and direction of travel will be named only by their initials throughout the rest of this book. It will be well for you to get the various combinations firmly in mind right away:

1. RI—Right inside
2. RO—Right outside
3. LI—Left inside
4. LO—Left outside
5. RFI—Right forward inside
6. RFO—Right forward outside
7. LFI—Left forward inside
8. LFO—Left forward outside
9. RBI—Right back inside
10. RBO—Right back outside
11. LBI—Left back inside
12. LBO—Left back outside

Until now, the instructions on how to position yourself while stroking or gliding have indicated the parts of your body in the traditional "right and left" way—for instance, "right shoulder," "left hip," and "right arm." Now, so there will be no confusion in explaining some highly technical movements, it is time to use just two terms when describing the body members. To do so, we need to run an imaginary line down your middle and divide you into two halves: the *skating side* and the *free side*.

So obvious are the terms that an explanation seems unnecessary. But just to get matters on the record, the half of your body that finds itself, even momentarily, above the blade on which you are riding is the skating side. Your free side is above the skate that is off the ice. Incidentally, in some areas, you'll hear the skating and free sides called the "employed" and "unemployed" sides.

As can be expected, the various body members also now become *skating* or *free* parts. The foot on which you are skating becomes your skating foot. Above are your skating leg, skating hip, and skating shoulder. Opposite are your free foot, free leg, free hip, and free shoulder. All, too—if you happen to live in one of the areas where the terms are used—can be designated as "employed" or "unemployed."

Finally, let's look to a bit of ice terminology that confuses many a beginner when he is first learning to skate backward edges. Suppose that you are instructed to travel backward with one arm extended *forward*. Where should you place the arm—forward along your line of travel, or forward in relation to your body?

The answer: forward in relation to your body. It should be extended out to the front of your chest or stomach. All skating directions as to the front or rear placement of hands, arms, face, and the such are made with the body in mind, not the direction of travel.

All right. That takes care of the preliminaries. Now out to the ice we go.

Inside Forward Edge

The inside forward is the simplest of the edges to master. Using the accompanying illustration as a guide, let's try it first on the right foot.

The skater is captured in the photograph as she is moving through the edge on her RFI. To catch up with her, take several strokes in a circling movement to the left and then, as you did when curving for the first time in Chapter Five, glide on both feet for a moment. During the glide, square your hips and shoulders to your curving path, doing so by pressing your right shoulder back and allowing your left to come forward. Check to see that hips and shoulders are also level. Then take a peek at your arms. Your left arm should be gracefully curved, with your elbow held at about waist level and your hand palm down. Your right arm should be straight and angling out behind you. Let the fingers on both hands relax, but do not permit your hands to droop at the wrists.

Once in position, slowly raise your left leg and extend it out behind you, bending the knee and pointing your toes toward the center of the imaginary circle being skated. Let your weight ride onto your skating leg so that you are leaning and gliding on your RFI. Hold the position for as long as you can. If all goes well, you will continue along a curving path to your left until you complete either part or all of a full circle.

INSIDE FORWARD EDGE

That's fine for a first attempt. Now let's start again, this time paying particular attention to a number of details that must be mastered if the inside forward is to be perfected.

First, your hips and shoulders: As you enter the edge, your momentum will always try to swing your hips and shoulders in the direction of the curve. If you allow this swing to occur, you will veer off course and head toward the center of the circle. You can eliminate all swing by pressing back steadily on your skating shoulder and holding your hips squared to your skating foot and its blade. Concentrate especially on your skating hip during your first edges. Press it forward and toward the center of the body, so much so that, as skaters say, it feels "hollowed out." It is a feeling impossible to describe, but you'll recognize it when you experience it.

Often, while holding the skating shoulder pressed back, a beginner will allow his free shoulder to swing far forward and across his body. This, too, must be avoided, for it sets up a swing away from the center of the circle and "flattens out" the curve.

Your free foot: Always position your free foot so that the heel is directly over the line being traced by your skating blade. Point your toes toward the center of the circle and make sure that you hold them well inside the tracing. Guard against ever allowing your free foot to wander across to the outside of the tracing. Once it gets away from you, it will act like the rudder on a ship and immediately point you toward the center of the circle.

Your skating leg and foot: Just as when stroking, bend your skating knee and ankle forward and then hold them steadily at the same angle of bend. Take care not to put too much lean on your RFI, for too much lean will pull your weight off the blade and push your skating hip out of position, with the result that you will head into the circle. You will need a bit of time to learn just how much lean is required. Practice will show you.

Your head: Look straight ahead along your line of travel when you begin stroking into the curve. Once on your RFI, however, turn your head so that you are looking across your free shoulder toward the center of the circle. In this way, you'll be able to follow the path you are skating and better hold to your course. But be sure not to turn your shoulders along with your head.

In the next days, as you practice the inside forward edge, you should dispense with the preliminary two-footed glide as soon as possible. Instead, position your shoulders, arms, and hips for the edge while at a standstill. Then, without moving them at all, push off and take five strokes. On the fifth, immediately go into the edge.

During the same practice sessions, of course, work should begin on the left inside forward edge. Though you will be riding on your left skate and traveling in the opposite direction—this time to the right—all pointers will remain the same. The left inside forward edge is a mirror image of its brother.

Outside Forward Edge

Skaters agree that the outside forward is the most important of the edges. It involves a pronounced sideways lean that requires both discipline and strength to master. As the late Maribel Vinson Owen remarks in her book, *The Fun of Figure Skating*, you will find all other maneuvers on ice easier to perform once you have perfected that lean.

As usual, though it may be skated on either blade, let's try the edge first on the right foot. As you did for the inside forward, gather speed with several strokes, this time along a curve to the right, and then enter the two-footed glide for a moment, using the time to assume your edge position.

The position is quite different from all that you have taken before. As the skater on page 82 has done, bring your right hip, shoulder, and arm to the front, simultaneously pressing your left hip, shoulder, and arm to the rear. All this will put your back toward the inside of the circle you are about to skate, with your shoulders roughly at a forty-five-degree angle to your line of travel. Angle your left arm out to the side behind you and place your right hand, palm down, about a foot in front of your stomach and just outside the line of the coming circle. Turn your head so that you are looking over your right shoulder and toward the center of the circle.

All set? Now raise your left skate clear of the ice and extend it to the rear for little more than a blade's length. Hold your knee straight but flexed, point your toes sharply outward, and place your

OUTSIDE FORWARD EDGE

instep directly over the line being traced by the blade. In the very same instant, shift your weight to your right skate and lean your whole body well into the circle; keep yourself "all in one piece" from the blade edge upward, but send yourself far over on your RFO. Concentrate on holding your shoulders level, your hips firm, and your back straight. Press back on your free hip and shoulder so that they are running parallel to your line of travel. Throughout, continue to look over your skating shoulder so that you can check your course and also keep tabs on the angle of your lean.

For as long as you hold the glide, you should travel in a wide curve. In fact, if you are like most beginners, you will curve far too wide, with your completed circle having a diameter of about twenty-five feet or so. At fault will be your natural tendency not to lean far enough to the side for fear of losing your balance. You will need to practice steadily through the next days—more likely through the next weeks—before building the confidence necessary to give you the deep lean that will tighten the circle to its proper diameter—a diameter that is about three times your height. But take heart. The confidence will come.

Now, as we did with the inside forward, let's try the edge again and look to those details that will help you perfect it.

Hips and shoulders: As usual, on entering the edge, you'll feel your momentum start to work against you, doing what it can to swing your hips and shoulders in the direction of the curve. Again, resist the swing. Firmly hold your shoulders parallel to your line of travel and constantly push back on your free hip. Otherwise, you'll find yourself heading toward the center of the circle.

Remember, too, that the hips must always remain level. Just as your free hip will want to swing forward with your momentum when you enter the curve, so will it want to rise when you lean to the side. You may be tempted to let it do so, for it will give you the feeling of pressing down more firmly on your skating blade. But it will shift your weight forward to the front part of the blade and may cause you to skid. For best balance and blade control, the outside forward should be performed on the back center area of the blade. This is the area on which you will automatically be riding if you correctly enter the curve.

Though your shoulders should also be level, you may allow the one on your skating side to "sink" just a bit, for it will be pulled down with the weight exerted by your lean. But do not allow it to drop significantly. By concentrating on keeping your shoulder line level, you will safeguard yourself from too great a "sink."

Finally, watch for any tendency to "poke" your skating hip toward the center of the circle. The hip may want to shove itself outward because of the weight exerted on it by your lean. If permitted a "poke," it will reduce your control over the skating blade. The whole problem can be avoided by sticking to that time-honored instruction: Lean "all in one piece."

Your free foot: With your momentum always trying to swing your body in the direction of the curve, you will need to pay special attention to your free foot. As with the inside forward—and for the same reason—never allow it to ride out beyond the tracing line. To combat any free-foot "swing," hold the knee above straight (but flexed) and firmly in place.

The forward outside should be practiced right from the start on both the right and the left foot, with all the advice just given also holding true for the left-footed version. Once you have gotten the "feel" of the edge by entering it from the two-footed glide, begin to work directly from a stroking action. Take the edge position while at a standstill, then stroke in an arc, and go into the edge on the fourth or fifth stroke.

Inside Backward Edge

You will be ready to experiment with the inside and outside backward edges once you have learned to skate backward with confidence. You may be wise, however, to delay matters a bit until you have the back crossover well in hand, for you will find the two edges much easier to enter from the crossover position. You may begin with one edge or the other, but many skaters will advise you to start with the inside version, claiming it to be the simpler to master. As usual, though it can be skated on either blade, we'll demonstrate it on the right foot.

The camera has caught the skater on page 85 as she is gliding through the edge. So that you can follow suit, carry yourself along a clockwise arc with four or five back crossovers and then settle into a glide on your RBI. You will find that the last crossover has, quite naturally, put you into the edge position.

Your free leg, with knee straight, will be extended to your rear, but it will be in the lead so far as your direction of travel is con-

INSIDE BACKWARD EDGE

cerned. Your toes will be aimed toward the center of the circle. Likewise, your stomach—for the crossover will have turned your hips and shoulders so that they are parallel with the skating blade below.

All you need do now is perform three tasks. First, keep your free hip pressed firmly back and your free leg perfectly straight so that neither will swing and send you off course. Second, turn your head and look over your free shoulder to see where you are going. And third, remain steadily on your RBI, doing so by leaning confidently into the circle. Do these three jobs and you'll find yourself gliding easily through the edge and back to your starting point.

One final point: For a look of complete grace while on the edge, develop the knack of holding your arms as the skater on page 85 is holding hers. Carry the skating arm, bent at the elbow, forward, and send the free arm out to the rear fully extended. This will position your shoulders across the line of your skating blade. When you first try the positioning, it may tend to pull your free hip forward. Practice and a steady backward pressure will soon teach the hip to stay in place.

Outside Backward Edge

The outside backward, too, is simple to perform—simple, that is, except for the placement of your hips.

The edge may be executed on either blade, but, as usual, the camera has caught the skater traveling on her right foot. And again, to follow suit, you need to take several back crossover strokes and then, as if you were pausing while planning to switch to a regular back stroke, glide on your RBO with your left foot on the ice just to your front. At this time, your hips, arms, and shoulders should be squared to your skating blade.

When you are ready to try the edge, carry your left leg to the rear, lifting your foot clear of the ice and pointing your toes toward the outside of the circle while keeping the center of the blade over the tracing. As your free leg comes back, send your free shoulder and arm around with it, at the same time pressing back on your skating arm and shoulder. In this position, your back will be put toward the circle. Let your head also turn so that you are charting your path across your free shoulder. Remain steadily on your RBO by leaning well into the circle.

Now for the difficult part. Throughout the edge, your hips should remain well squared to the skating blade beneath. Though arms, hips, shoulders, and head all must change position, the hips must not be allowed to join them. And, thanks to all the other

OUTSIDE BACKWARD EDGE

movement and your momentum, they will want to do just *that*. You must hold them in check by exerting a strong and unrelenting forward pressure on your free hip. You can help yourself to do so by tightening the muscles in your buttocks in the instant that your free leg begins its swing to the back. Then, throughout the edge, refuse to loosen them. If you permit the hips to turn, they will aim your free leg into the circle and possibly set you to skidding.

As with the outside forward, the importance of your lean into the circle must always be emphasized. Lean strongly, confident that your blade edge will bite efficiently into the ice. Feel your weight pressing against your skating shoulder, and allow the shoulder to "sink" with it a little. If you try to hold your shoulders level, you will pull your body up from the circle and "flatten" the curve or send yourself into a sideways skid.

Since both the inside and outside backward edges can be performed on either foot, you should begin immediately to practice them on the left foot. Though you must become equally adept at both the inside and outside versions, you may want to give a shade more attention to the latter before you are done; for, if you plan to go on to actual figure skating, you will soon find that a great many freestyle jumps bring the skater back down to the ice on his RBO or LBO edges.

Whether your goal is the most accomplished general skating possible or actual figure work, you have taken a long stride forward by learning to glide through the four basic edges. To your general skating abilities you have added much variety and, as a result, much fun. As for actual figures, you've come to within one step of beginning work on them. All that remains is to learn one last basic skill —a skill that can be called "interrupting your circles."

EIGHT

Adding Skill: Interrupted Circles

This final basic skill, this "interrupting your circles," is divided into two movements: the *turn* on the curve, and the *roll*. With the first, you will be able to do an about-face at any point along the curve without changing your direction of travel. The latter will carry you over the ice—all the way from one end of the rink to the other if you so please—in a series of half circles. The roll, incidentally, is known by a variety of names. It is quite often called the "consecutive edge," the "half circle," or the "half circle swing."

Since you've already tried a simple turn while skating in a straight line (Chapter Five), let's first learn how to interrupt a circle with the turn.

Turning on the Curve

You may turn on the curve with either of two actions: the *mohawk*, or the *three-turn*. Each may be used to swing you from front to back or from back to front. Each may be skated on a right or a left curve. But each is much different from the other, for the mohawk is made with both feet, and the three-turn with just one.

The Inside Forward Mohawk

The mohawk comes by its name because it resembles an action seen in the war dances of America's early Mohawk Indians. Depending on the skating actions involved during the turn, it breaks down into several types. Of the lot, the simplest to learn is the *inside forward* version.

The inside forward mohawk—you'll usually hear it called "the inside mohawk" or even just "the mohawk" at the rink—carries you from riding forward on the inside edge of one blade to sailing along backward on the inside edge of the other blade. The turn may be entered on either foot, but is most commonly made from the right to the left foot. This is the manner in which we shall first try it, after which you can reverse the whole process and experiment with the left entry.

For your first attempt, gather a little forward speed with several strokes and then glide along the inside forward edge. Everything should be as usual for the edge: hips and shoulders squared to your blade, skating knee bent, free left leg back (and also bent), and foot of the free skate pointing its toes toward the interior of the circle.

Now, with the skater pictured opposite, carry your left foot forward until it is alongside the foot opposite. But bring it forward heel first and then allow the heel almost to touch the instep of your skating foot.

You are now ready for the turn itself. To begin turning yourself around, first lower your left skate to the ice, where it will find itself moving backward along your line of travel. As soon as it touches the ice, shift your weight to it and allow your right skate to slide out to the front along your curving path. At the very same time, swing your shoulders so that the left one rides forward of your body and the right presses back. With these movements, you should look exactly like the skater on page 92.

Now smartly turn yourself so that your back is to your line of travel. You will be gliding backward on your left inside edge. Bring your right skate clear of the ice and hold it there for as long as you wish to go on gliding as you are. As usual when skating any of the edges, look across your free shoulder to chart your path.

One pointer: While you certainly may take your time in preparing for the turn, you must then swing yourself about quickly and smartly. If you hesitate once you've started to turn yourself—or if you try to make the turn slowly—you are apt to skid or stumble. And, even if you manage to avoid these problems, your mohawk is bound to look awkward.

PREPARED POSITION FOR INSIDE MOHAWK

Outside Backward Mohawk

Thanks to the forward inside mohawk, you're now turned completely front to back. But suppose that you wish to swing around again so that you are once more riding forward along your curving path. Here you can use another very common mohawk action: the *outside backward*.

This mohawk, which will carry you from the outside edge of one blade to the outside edge of its companion, can be entered on the

TURNING IN THE MOHAWK

right or the left foot. To demonstrate it on the right foot, let's go back to the point where you completed the inside forward action.

Gliding along backward on your LI as you are, you need return your right foot to the ice, shift your weight to it so that you are on its outside edge, and hold the position as seen below.

Now, as the skater is doing on the next page, lift your left foot and swing it out to the side in an arc that will carry it back behind your right skate. Swing your arms and your upper body right along with it.

GLIDING POSITION FOR OUTSIDE BACKWARD MOHAWK

As your left skate makes its swing, point your toes outward and turn the foot so that, at the end of its arc, it is aimed along your path of travel, just as it is doing on page 95. When the foot strikes the ice, shift your weight to it and send yourself . . .

. . . gliding along a forward path on your LO with your back to the circle. Lift your right leg from the ice and continue your glide along the circle.

These two actions—the inside forward and the outside back-

LEFT LEG SWINGING ON OUTSIDE BACKWARD MOHAWK

ward—will really be all the mohawk turns that you will ever need for general skating. Several of their relatives, among them the *forward outside open* and *closed mohawks*, are used principally in ice dancing and require a great deal of skill to perform. Should you take up ice dancing seriously and plan to enter competition, you will need to work under an instructor. With his help, you will be able to learn all the advanced mohawks.

LEFT FOOT ON ICE BEHIND RIGHT IN OUTSIDE BACKWARD MOHAWK

The Three-Turn

The three-turn is a turn made on one foot, either the right or the left, while skating forward or backward along a curve. Often simply called the *three,* it takes its name from the fact that the blade leaves etched behind on the ice a pattern resembling the numeral 3. When skillfully performed, it is one of the most graceful maneuvers in skating.

Every three-turn begins on one edge of the blade in use and ends on the edge opposite. In between, the skater smartly executes a pivot. Along with the mohawk, the three-turn divides itself into several types. The most commonly used of all is the *outside forward three-turn,* which leaves the following pattern on the ice when skated on the right foot:

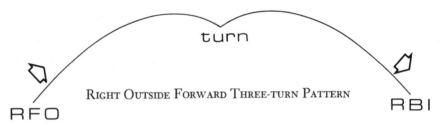

RIGHT OUTSIDE FORWARD THREE-TURN PATTERN

To trace this pattern with your own blade, take several forward strokes along a clockwise curve and then glide on your RO, with your left foot out behind you and off the ice. Lean toward the center of the circle being skated and carry your weight so that you are riding on the back center area of your blade. Hold your hips squared to your skating blade, but let your right shoulder come forward and your left shoulder go back.

Now, with the skater opposite, bring your free foot into a T position just off the ice and directly behind your right skate. At the same time, reverse the position of your shoulders, bringing your left shoulder around toward the center of the circle and pressing back on your right shoulder. Do not, however, let your hips swing around with them.

Once in this position, you are prepared for the three-turn. Your weight must now come forward a little so that it shifts from the back center of the blade to the front center. Got it? Good. Now pivot to the right along with the skater in the photograph. The camera has caught her about midway through the turn.

Continue the pivot all the way around until your back is to your line of travel. Throughout, keep your free skate off the ice and behind your skating foot. As soon as you complete the turn, reverse the pressure on your shoulders. You will go gliding backward along the curve on your RI, the exact copy of the skater in the photograph on the next page.

PREPARED POSITION FOR RIGHT OUTSIDE FORWARD THREE-TURN

Now for some pointers: First, when preparing for the turn, bring your left shoulder around toward the center of the circle *strongly* and press back *hard* on your right shoulder. To help matters along, look toward the center of the circle. If brought around strongly and far enough, your shoulders will make the pivoting action quite easy. But if you swing them halfheartedly, you will not exert enough pressure on the skating blade for a good turn. You will end up having to try a sort of jumping movement to get yourself faced about.

PIVOT ON RIGHT OUTSIDE FORWARD THREE-TURN

But never allow the hips to come around with the shoulders. Lock them firmly in place, for, if they begin to swing at any time before, during, or after the pivot, they will set up a spinning action that will send you into a skid.

Your skating knee, of course, will be bent forward as you glide prior to the turn. But when you bring your free foot into the T position, straighten the skating leg and hold it firm throughout the turn. As for the free foot, always keep it behind the skating foot. It may want to fly out to the side with the pivoting action. You're in

GLIDE AFTER RIGHT OUTSIDE FORWARD THREE-TURN

for trouble if it does. It can put you into a spin that is almost guaranteed to sit you down hard on the ice.

Once you have learned to skate the right outside forward three-turn, you can apply the process to skating all of its relatives: outside forward to the left, inside forward to the right and left, and backward to the right and left. The pointers given above will hold true for each maneuver.

Should you go in for figure work or ice dancing, you will encounter what is known as the *forward outside waltz three*. To perform it, you execute the three-turn in its usual way, but then, after gliding backward for a moment, you bring your free foot to the ice and switch to riding on it. The turn is otherwise known as the *drop three* because the free foot is "dropped" to the ice on the backward glide.

Four Rolls

Rolls are a series of half circles made along the ice on one foot and then the other. Along with the basic edges, they are skated in two directions: forward on the outside or the inside edge, and backward on the outside or the inside edge.

To get a beginning idea of how these half circles will look when skated, draw an imaginary line along the ice and call it the *long axis*. Now envision a series of half circles spaced along both sides of the line, with every other one to the right and the intervening ones to the left. In all, the pattern will look like this:

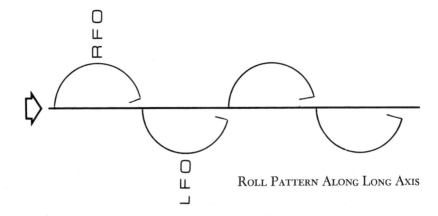

Roll Pattern Along Long Axis

The diagram, though it is intended to give you a general idea of the roll pattern, actually shows the half circles as they look when you skate the outside forward roll. You will notice that each half circle ends in a little bend of the line; you'll see the reason for this in a moment. Let's see now if we can trace this exact pattern with the outside forward roll.

Outside and Inside Forward Rolls

Though the outside forward roll can be started on either foot, we'll begin on the right foot as usual, with the understanding that the process will simply be reversed when you experiment with the left. At a standstill, set yourself in the T position, placing your right skate ahead and putting its toe directly on the long axis and at right angles to it. Now, with your hips squared to your planned line of travel but with your right shoulder forward (so that your back is to the coming circle, just as if you are going to skate an outside forward edge), gently push off and glide along a clockwise curve on your RFO. Let your free foot come off the ice behind you. You should be an exact copy of the skater in the photograph on page 102.

As you glide, count slowly to three. The count should carry you about a quarter distance of the half circle. Now slowly swing your free skate forward and let it ride past your skating foot until it is extended out in front of you. As it is moving, begin to reverse your shoulder position, bringing your left shoulder forward and pressing back on your right. They should be in the neutral position at the same time your free skate passes your skating foot. Then they should continue moving until they are facing you toward the center of the circle. At last, you should be in the position shown on page 103. Your skating knee should now be straight, having come out of its original bend to give the free skate sufficient clearance to complete its swing without hitting the ice.

This position should now be held for three counts. You will glide around the half circle and will start coming back to the long axis. As you approach the long axis, let your free foot drop back alongside your skating foot. When the skates are parallel, gently place the free blade on the ice as shown on page 104. Then bend both knees.

PUSHOFF FOR OUTSIDE FORWARD ROLL

Now turn your right foot outward as if readying yourself for a new stroke—which is exactly what you're planning to do. (This movement accounts for the little bend at the end of each half circle in the roll diagram.) As you come up to the long axis, stroke with your right foot and let yourself ride onto your LFO. As pictured on page 105, you'll be moving into your next half circle.

Once into the new half circle, you need now only repeat all the

FREE LEG FORWARD AND SHOULDERS ROTATED IN
FORWARD OUTSIDE ROLL

movements, but this time, of course, in reverse, after which you return to your original actions for the third half circle. Incidentally,
you need not reset your shoulders at the beginning of each new
half circle. Just keep them as they were once you had faced into the
previous half circle. Quite naturally, they will now be facing away
from the new half circle.

FEET TOGETHER AND KNEES BENT NEAR END OF OUTSIDE
FORWARD ROLL

Two pointers: First, take particular care not to let your free hip
ride forward as you carry your free leg past your skating leg and extend it to your front. It should remain squared to your skating
blade right from pushoff; if it comes forward, you can expect the
usual spinning action that may cause a skid. You can help keep the
hip where it belongs by carrying your free leg quite close past the

GLIDING INTO NEW HALF CIRCLE ON FORWARD OUTSIDE ROLL

skating leg. A close passing movement will also help you maintain a proper lean into the circle.

Second, when you are ready for a fresh stroke at the end of each half circle, be sure to turn your thrusting foot out a full quarter turn. It will then thrust you at right angles across the long axis, making it easy for you to describe a well-rounded new half circle. If the foot is not turned sufficiently far out, you will likely pass across the axis line at a slant, with the result that you will describe a too-shallow half circle.

Once you have gotten the knack of the outside forward roll, you will find its brother—the inside forward—quite easy to perform.

Free Leg Extended on Inside Forward Roll

For the inside forward roll, push off and glide on your RFI just as you would for an inside forward edge. Count to three and then slowly swing your free leg forward, at the same time turning your shoulders so that you are facing somewhat toward the center of the circle. As before, however, keep your hips squared to your skating blade. Let the free leg ride out to your front, with toes pointing along your curving path.

Hold this glide for another three count, after which your free foot comes back and to the ice alongside your skating foot. Turn the skating foot outward and thrust yourself onto your LFI when you reach the axis line. Then, reversing the above movements, sail through the second half circle.

Just as promised, it was quite easy to perform, wasn't it?

But just one pointer: On both the inside and outside forward rolls, be sure to lean back a little while your free leg is extended to your front. By doing so, you will counterbalance the weight exerted by your suspended leg.

Outside and Inside Backward Rolls

It's time to draw another diagram on the ice.

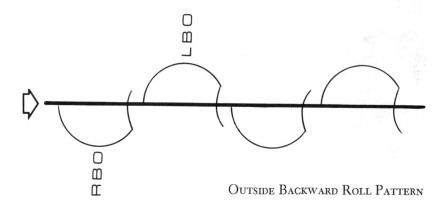

OUTSIDE BACKWARD ROLL PATTERN

This is the pattern that you will skate as, after starting on your right foot, you execute a series of outside backward rolls. During each half circle, you will glide much as you did when trying the outside back edges. You will, however, enter the roll much differently.

FEET COMING TOGETHER FOR PUSHOFF INTO OUTSIDE BACK ROLL

You were able to approach the edge on a back crossover, but for the roll you will need to push off from a standstill.

Let's first see how that pushoff is made, following then with a description of the roll itself. To begin, stand so that you are facing along the axis line. Your feet should be parallel to each other, with the right skate on the line itself and the left skate about eighteen inches or so away. Put your weight on your left skate and then,

PIVOTING FOR START OF OUTSIDE BACK ROLL

with the skater shown in the opposite photograph, carry your right skate over to it, bending your knees deeply as you do so.

Immediately—before the right skate has a chance to touch the ice—pivot to the right on your left skate. Simultaneously, straighten your left knee and push against your LBI. Your body will describe a quarter turn and begin to move.

As the pivot is completed, lower your right foot to the ice.

Turned and in motion as you are, your right toe should come down on the axis line and at a right angle to it. When the right skate touches the ice, shift your weight to it and lean onto your RBO. You will now be riding backward with your right knee deeply bent, while your left foot slides out to your front and comes up a few inches off the ice.

With your right knee bent, you will be gliding in a sort of "sit-

BEGINNING GLIDE ON RIGHT OUTSIDE BACK ROLL

ting position." Hold the position for a count of three. During this time, your hips should be squared to your skating blade, your left arm should be forward and your right arm back, and your face should be turned to see where you are going. At the end of the count, straighten your right leg and reverse your shoulders so that you put your back to the half circle. Continue gliding until you curve around and begin heading back toward the long axis.

THRUST ON RIGHT OUTSIDE BACK ROLL

Now let your left leg swing down from its position to your front, and carry it past your skating leg to your rear. As you come up to the axis line, lower your left skate to the ice and, as the skater is doing on page 111, thrust yourself along with your right foot. Your weight will transfer itself to the outside edge of your left skate.

At the end of the thrust, slide your right foot to your front and bring it up from the ice. You will now glide into the second half circle. As you curve, reverse your shoulders so that your back is again to the half circle. Then swing your right leg to the rear and transfer your weight to it just before you enter the third half circle. All that remains to be done is to continue these actions until you reach the end of the long axis.

Once you have come to the end of the long axis, let's turn around and proceed back in the opposite direction, this time using the right inside backward roll.

To perform this roll, again you must position yourself at a standstill, but this time with your back to the axis line. Let your left skate rest on the line while placing your right skate about eighteen inches out to the side. Send your weight to the left blade and bring your right foot over to it.

While the skate is traveling over, allow your arms to move a little to the left. But as soon as it arrives, describe a semicircular thrust with your opposite foot and swing your arms back to your right. These movements will cause you to pivot and begin moving backward into the first half circle. Immediately put your right skate on the ice and transfer your weight to its inside edge. Let your left skate slide out to your front and leave the ice. You'll now look like the skater on page 113.

Continue to glide in this fashion for a moment, and then swing your free leg back in alongside your right. Hold it off the ice for a moment, and use the time to turn your shoulders so that you are looking into the half circle. As you come around the curve and head back to the axis line, let your left leg ride out a little behind you. Now get ready to change skating feet so that you can begin the next half circle.

SKATER ON RI AT BEGINNING OF INSIDE BACK ROLL

The change here is quite different from those made in the other rolls or in the basic edges. Bring your left foot forward alongside your right, and then turn the left heel out as far as possible. In the next instant, execute a sculling action with your right foot. The sculling action will thrust you toward the axis line, after which your left skate should come down to the ice. You will be in the position shown in the photograph on page 114.

SCULLING ACTION ON RIGHT BACK INSIDE ROLL

Once your left skate is on the ice, shift your weight to its inside edge, carry your right foot out to your front, and glide along the beginning path of the second half circle. Now, to get through this new curve and the ones that follow, repeat all the actions, gliding on and thrusting with the appropriate feet and turning your shoulders so that you can look into the half circle.

One pointer: On both the inside and outside backward rolls, take great care to keep your hips always squared to your skating blade. You will be much tempted to swing the skating hip on the stroke that occurs near the end of the outside roll—and even more tempted to do so on the sculling movement needed for the inside version. Practice always to keep that hip tucked firmly in place.

A FINAL NOTE: PRACTICE

Oh, boy! We've learned a great many skating actions between the time when you tried your first forward strokes in Chapter Three and this moment when you have come to the end of your first interrupted circles. Throughout, there have been numerous reminders to practice each maneuver until you have it down pat.

If you have been taking the time to practice, you have already come up against a basic problem in ice skating. Every maneuver involves so many details of body placement that it seems impossible to keep them all in mind at the same time. While practicing an edge or a roll, who can remember all at once: Keep my hip tucked in, turn my shoulders, lean on my outside edge, hold my skating knee bent, point my free skate to the outside of circle, look to the center of the circle, and now change skating feet?

No one can, of course—but a great many young skaters never think of this truth. They try to keep every detail in mind for every minute of the time. As a result, they concentrate so hard on the details that they lose track of the maneuver itself. Confusion and mistakes mount, and all the fun soon goes out of skating.

There is no need whatsoever for you to join them. As you practice, do your best on every maneuver, of course. But work on one detail at a time. Practice turning your shoulders at one time; then concentrate on your hips, then on the bend of your skating knee and ankle, then on the manner in which your free foot should be pointed. Don't worry if you make some other mistake at the time. You'll soon take care of it.

Skating has been described as a "muscle memory" sport. Each muscle or set of muscles must be patiently taught what it is supposed to do during a given action. Once taught, it will "remember" and automatically behave properly in the future, and you will then be free to teach another set its responsibilities. By the time you're done—and it won't take long to train each group—you will be going through the maneuvers without consciously thinking of every little detail. Your "muscle memory" will be taking care of the details for you. So take your time. Attend to one matter at a time. You'll enjoy yourself all the more—and reach expert status all the sooner.

As promised, we come to the end of the skating basics with the four rolls. Now you are completely equipped to give as much variety as is possible to your pleasure skating; up and down the rink you can go for years to come, attempting all sorts of different movements. And now, if you are of a mind to go in for competitive figure skating, you have only to turn to the next page to see the excitement that lies ahead.

NINE

For the Competitor: Figure Skating

As soon as you decide to go in for competitive figure skating, you will find it a sport that is divided into two main branches: *school figures* and *freestyle*. When you participate in school figures events, you are required to skate circles in various combinations and in certain prescribed manners. In freestyle, you are permitted to blend a number of movements—from spins to jumps—into a skating routine lasting several minutes.

You should become as adept as possible in both school figures and freestyle skating, for you may not limit yourself to one or the other in any recognized competition (though there is presently talk of splitting them into separate events at some time in the future). A *program* (the skater's term for a series of school figures or a freestyle routine) in each must be presented. You will receive points for your performance in each, after which the points will be combined to give you an over-all total. With such scoring, you have a chance to win, singly or in any combination, the school figure event, the freestyle competition, and the best over-all performance award.

Here in our country, all figure skating competition is governed by the rules of the United States Figure Skating Association (USFSA). Competition begins at the local level and advances through sectional and regional championships to national championships. You may participate in these various meets as an individual member of the USFSA or as a member of an Association-approved club or school skating team. Many rinks form clubs for their skaters who wish to go in for competition. Age is no barrier for entry into the sport. All you need do is skate with sufficient skill to qualify for the competitions.

By participating in American meets, you may qualify for international competitions and the loftiest goals to which a figure skater can aspire: world and Olympic championships. International meets are regulated by the International Skating Union (ISU). The USFSA and other national associations that compete on a worldwide scale are members of the ISU. The basic rules for figure skating in international contests are the same as those on the national level.

One point must be emphasized before we talk further of competitive skating. You can very successfully teach yourself to skate if you plan to sail around the ice for pleasure only. But you will be unwise to prepare for competitive skating by yourself. You should have a coach, and you should work under his direction at all times.

Why? Competitive skating is one of the most demanding of sports. It leaves little or no room for error in the execution of both school figures and freestyle movements. If you attempt to teach yourself, you will run a great risk of allowing mistakes and weaknesses to creep into your skating style and become a lasting part of it. They can keep you from ever developing into a champion. But with an expert coach at your side, they can be quickly seen and corrected. Your local rink will be happy to advise you on the best coaches available in your vicinity.

Because figure skating is such an exacting sport, we must approach this part of the book in a manner different from that used in the past. In the previous chapters, instructions were given on how best to skate each new maneuver. Now, so there will not be the slightest chance for a damaging error to slip in through misunderstanding, we'll have to keep away from all instructional tips. We'll have to limit ourselves just to picturing and describing representative school figures and freestyle movements, leaving the job of teaching to your coach. In this way, you will be able to use this book to acquaint yourself with the sport, after which you can begin to develop your skill under your coach's watchful eye. In all, you should then be in fine shape for future competition.

Now let's begin with the school figures.

THE SCHOOL FIGURES

The skating of the school figures—which are also known as *compulsory figures*—has often been called "drawing on ice by using your blade as a pen." Left on the ice are tracings of circles in various combinations of two and three. In all, there are nineteen such combinations, but since most can be executed on either foot and while traveling either forward or backward, the school figures are said to total seventy. Of those seventy figures, some are quite easy to skate, while others are clear over on the difficult side.

You should plan to learn all the school figures if you hope to become a first-rank competitor. As you climb toward your dream of a national or an international championship, you will need to qualify for each new meet by showing your ability to skate figures of increasing difficulty.

Your ability can be checked by a series of tests conducted under the auspices of the USFSA. Numbering nine in all, they begin with a preliminary test and end with what is called the Eighth, or Gold, Test. The simplest of the school figures, of course, are checked in the earliest tests, and the most difficult in the Eighth. Each test must be passed before the next in line can be taken. Various emblems are awarded for passing the tests. They range from a pin won for the preliminary test to a gold medal, gold bar, or ribbon for the Eighth Test.

From your very first days of practice, you should be aware of how you will be scored when you enter competition. Scoring is based on the difficulty of the figure being skated, with the more difficult figures always promising a bigger score. To give you your final points, a panel of judges combine two methods of computation. First, each figure is assigned a *factor*—a number designating the degree of difficulty posed by the figure. The factor numbers run from 1 to 6. The simplest figures have a factor of 1, and the most difficult a factor of 6.

Next, each figure is judged on the basis of the technical skill and personal style with which it is performed. The numbers o through 6 are used at this point. They indicate the following:

> o—figure not skated
> 1—bad performance
> 2—poor performance
> 3—average performance
> 4—good performance
> 5—excellent performance
> 6—perfect performance

At the end of your performance, each judge will multiply your performance number by your factor number. For instance, if a judge thinks that you have performed a 1-factor figure without a fault, your score will be 6. He may also modify your score with the use of decimal points; if he thinks that your performance has been somewhere between "good" and "excellent," he may award you such marks as 4.3 or 4.5. The scores given by all the judges are then reviewed and are used as the basis for determining your placement in the competition. You may win. Or you may place second or third, or farther down the line.

As was said just a moment ago, your execution of a figure is judged on your technical skill and your personal style. Both are governed by rules that you must follow if you hope to earn high marks. These rules are to be found in detail in *The USFSA Rulebook*. Before ever entering competition, you will want to study them closely—even memorize them—exactly as they are written in the *Rulebook*. But to help you get started, here they are in brief:

Technical Skill

1. You must begin each figure from a standstill. The figure should begin with a single stroke from your blade edge. The toe picks must not be used to set you in motion, nor should you get

under way with any unnecessary or exaggerated movements of the body.

2. Your first stroke must be made at the intersecting point of two of the circles to be skated. Then you must skate the figure three times on each foot, doing so without pause.

3. As you skate, you must maintain the long and transverse axes of your figure. You already know the meaning of the long axis. The transverse axis is an imaginary line that runs at right angles to the long axis and passes through it at the point where the circles intersect. By continually maintaining these axes, each of your circles will remain the same size and in the same place for as long as you repeat the figure. No circle will tend to "drift away" from where it belongs.

4. All your circles must be of equal size and must intersect properly.

5. The lines traced in the ice by your blade must be as steady as possible. If your first tracing is faulty, wavering, or off course, you must correct it on your next trip around. Do not make the mistake of traveling right back over the faulty lines in the hope that the judges will be impressed by your accuracy. They will only lower your score.

Skating Style

The USFSA Rulebook advises that all exaggerations of body movement and position be persistently avoided if your tally for style is to be high. Your aim is a graceful and flowing presentation that will cause the viewer to murmur, "My, that looks easy." An appearance of effortlessness is one of the hallmarks of any truly masterful and artistic performance, as you well know if you have watched an excellent dancer, actor, or pantomimist at work. To help you to such a performance, the Rulebook sets the following style rules:

1. Your carriage should be one that holds the upper part of the body and the head easily and naturally erect. Your upper body should neither bend forward nor lean to the side from the hips.

2. Your arms should be held easily, with your hands set no higher than the waist. Your palms should be held easily and parallel to the ice, while your fingers should be together in a natural fashion, neither stiffly extended nor clenched. Just let them curve slightly at the knuckles.

3. Your skating leg should always have a slight and elastic bend at the knee.

4. Likewise, your free knee should be bent, but slightly so, and held generally over the tracing line. When to your front, the free leg is best held with the knee and ankle gracefully extended.

5. As for your free foot, it should be held just above the ice. It should be pointed downward and outward.

As was said earlier, you will want to study and memorize these tips direct from the *Rulebook* so that they will remain firmly in mind not only while you are actually competing but all the while you are practicing. When practicing, you will, of course, need to work just as though you were on the ice during a meet, with hundreds of eyes on you. For, as an experienced skater once aptly put it, "As you practice, so will you skate."

The seventy school figures are all to be found diagramed in the *Rulebook*. These diagrams should be studied as closely as the technical and style rules so that, from the very moment you first try any figure, you will have a vivid mental picture of the tracing to be left on the ice. There is no need to repeat all the diagrams here, for your coach will always have available a copy of the *Rulebook* for you to see, and so let's get acquainted with the figures by looking at just a representative few of their patterns—four in all.

The first of the four will give you a firm idea of how a figure is basically skated. The remaining three will indicate just how varied the figures are.

Circle Eight

The first pattern is the simple *circle eight*. It can be skated in four ways, and thus serves as the basis for the initial four of the seventy school figures. When traced on the ice, it looks like the figure opposite.

The four ways in which it can be skated are: (1) RFO-LFO

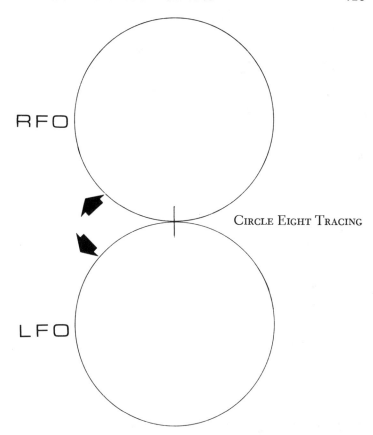

RFO

LFO

CIRCLE EIGHT TRACING

(right forward outside edge to left forward outside edge), (2) RFI-LFI, (3) RBO-LBO, and (4) RBI-LBI. The first two ways each have a scoring factor of 1, the latter two a factor of 2. When going through the nine USFSA figure tests, you will need to skate the first three in the First Test, while reserving the fourth for the Second Test.

Now, using the diagram on page 124 as a guide, let's see how the figure is skated. We'll skate it RFO-LFO.

You push off from the point where the two circles intersect, and glide through the first circle on your RFO. Your left leg is carried behind you until you begin to curve back toward the intersecting point, at which time you swing the leg to your front. Then, at the intersecting point, the left skate drops to the ice and alongside your right one. You thrust forward with the right skate and glide

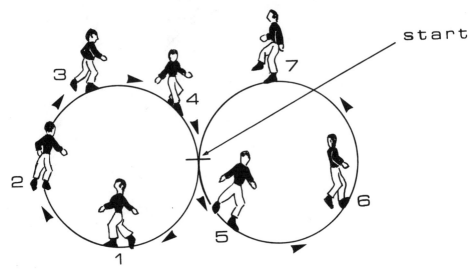

start

CIRCLE EIGHT WITH SKATER DRAWN IN AT GIVEN POINTS IN FIGURE

through the second circle on your LFO. The right foot trails gracefully behind for most of the circle and then comes forward as you again approach the intersecting point.

Please note the position of the shoulders in the diagram. See how they face you to the outside as you enter each circle and then rotate so that you are looking inward as you return to the intersecting point.

Varied Patterns

Now, to understand just how varied the school figures can be, look to the three patterns opposite. The name and tracing of each pattern are shown, along with the different ways in which each can be skated. Remember, each way counts as one school figure. Also shown are the scoring factors and the number of the USFSA test in which the figures must be skated. The figures are (1) the *three*, (2) the *change double three*, and (3) the *paragraph loop*.

In both the *three* and the *change double three* patterns, three-turns put in an appearance at specified points. And when you try the change double three, you will find that each skate must go from one blade edge to the other before the pattern is completed. Not

TEST: 1   3   8

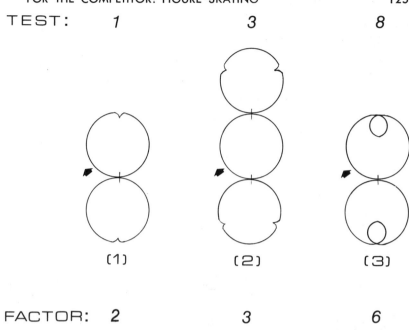

           (1)   (2)   (3)

FACTOR: 2   3   6

THREE PATTERNS: 1. THREE; 2. CHANGE DOUBLE THREE;
3. PARAGRAPH LOOP

only are the seventy figures varied, but also the movements within them.

To the spectator who is not familiar with the intricacies of skating, the variations among and within the figures are hard to see. Consequently, as he sits in the gallery during a meet, he is likely to find the school figures a boring business. You may well share his feelings at the start, but you can count on having your mind soon changed. You'll never feel the same again once you have learned to skate the school figures and have come to know the challenge that they constantly pose for your skill.

But now let's turn to the branch of the sport that never fails to excite all concerned, spectator and skater alike: freestyle skating.

FREESTYLE SKATING

When in freestyle competition, you will need to present a nicely balanced program of such movements as jumps, spins, spirals, dance steps, and variations of the school figures. Throughout, you should attempt to skate on one foot or the other as much as possible, keeping all two-footed skating at a minimum. At most meets, you can count on being on the ice for about five minutes. Your program will be skated to a music of your choosing.

Freestyle skating has long been known as the "creative" half of figure competition. Here, you can let your imagination take over, combining your movements as you wish and setting them to a music that befits your mood. In some competitions, you may choose all your movements for yourself. In others, certain specified movements must be included. But in all cases, they may be put in any order that you desire and then be skated in the manner that best suits your personality, your individuality. Your performance

THE SPIRAL

may be fiery, sprightly, or serene—anything that reflects you as you really are. Or it may change mood at any time. It all depends on your imagination.

Your program will be judged along a scoring scale of o to 6 for technical merit, program composition, and your skating style. Judging for technical merit goes into such areas as the difficulty of the movements executed, their variety, and the sureness and skill with which you skate them.

To earn high marks for program composition and skating style, you will need to keep a number of pointers in mind. First, you will want to combine your various movements in the most original way possible and then have them flow from one to another smoothly. You will want them to harmonize with the music and be always in time with it. You will want to skate over as much of the rink space as you can so that your movements will be clearly seen at their flowing best. And you will want to carry yourself with the utmost ease and grace from the moment you glide onto the ice.

The freestyle movements are many and even more varied than the school figures. All are exciting to watch and perform. The ones that we shall now see are known as the basic movements. They will serve as the foundation for your freestyle work and will open the way to more daring and complex maneuvers.

The Spiral

The *spiral* is a freestyle movement that carries you over the ice on one leg or the other while you are bent forward at the waist with your arms outspread and your free leg riding high behind you. You may ride in a straight line or along a curve with the spiral. And you may enter the movement while skating forward or backward. It is felt to be one of the most graceful of the freestyle actions.

The Spin

On page 128, the skater is performing the *one-foot spin*, while on page 129 she has lowered herself to the *sit spin*.

Both movements set the skater to whirling around and around while standing in one place on the ice. The one-foot spin begins

STANDING SPIN

with the free foot just below the skating knee, as seen in the photograph. But after a moment or so, the free foot is pressed down and across the skating foot to give the spin greater speed.

Most skaters agree that, regardless of all its whirling action, the spin is relatively easy to perform while standing. You will very likely meet it early in your training, with your coach first instructing you in a very simple two-foot version. Very soon, you'll be working on one foot and then learning how to drop into the sit spin, sending your free leg forward so that you resemble a Russian dancer.

Later you will have the chance to master the *camel*, a spin per-

SIT SPIN

formed while you are holding the spiral position. Finally, the day will come when you can try the *flying camel* and the *flying sit spin*. Breathtaking to watch, both are spins that are entered from leaps.

The Pivot

With the *pivot*, you turn yourself into a human version of a draftsman's compass. The toe picks hold one skate firmly in place beneath you while you spin round and let your other skate print a tight circle in the ice.

You may perform this action while spinning to the front or the

FORWARD INSIDE PIVOT

rear. A pivot to the front is called a *forward inside pivot*; in reverse, it becomes a *back inside pivot*. At all times, the leg above the "holding" skate must be strongly bent, while its companion is always gracefully extended.

The Spread Eagle

Here are two versions of still another of the freestyle skater's most breathtaking movements: the *spread eagle*. The maneuver

OUTSIDE SPREAD EAGLE   INSIDE SPREAD EAGLE

sends you around in a circle with your feet widely spread and your
heels pointing toward each other.

In the picture on the left, the skater has her back to the circle
and is performing an outside spread eagle. In the companion picture, she is traveling through an *inside spread eagle*. The lean
needed for a good spread eagle must always be deep and strong.

Jumps

Freestyle skating is spiced with a wide variety of jumps, the simplest of their number being the *bunny hop*. While skating forward, you spring into the air from the toe of your left skate, stretch your right leg far forward, and land on the toe of your right skate. Then you push forward with your right toe, change to a left-footed glide, and go sailing on along the ice.

BUNNY HOP

The bunny hop will probably be the first on your list of jumps to be mastered. Next will come the *waltz jump,* which looks a bit like the bunny hop while you are in the air. You will, however, fly higher and then make a half turn so that, when you land, you will be traveling backward.

Then it will be time to try the *mazurka.*

The mazurka is a jump that turns you from skating backward to forward along your path of travel. You need to tap the toe of your

MAZURKA JUMP

right skate on the ice, leap into the air with ankles crossed and arms outstretched, execute a half turn, and land on your right skate, after which you push into a left-footed glide.

In the photograph on page 133, the skater, looking much like a ballet dancer, has her right ankle crossed in front of her left. This is the traditional midair position for the jump, but the mazurka can be varied so that left ankle is to the front. If performed strongly, this variation is called the *scissors jump*.

Soon cropping up on your list of jumps will be the *toe loop* and the *loop*. Each is entered while skating backward. Each requires a full turn while you are in the air. And each lands you still moving backward along your line of travel. Though the two jumps are much alike, they are different in one respect. The toe of one skate is used to help you into the air in the toe loop. It plays no part in the loop.

While mastering the loops, you will undoubtedly try your first *salchow*. Pronounced "sal-cow" here in the United States, it is a jump that is named after its inventor, the champion skater Ulrich Salchow. It is a jump that carries you from skating backward on the inside edge of your left blade to skating backward on the outside edge of your right blade.

It is impossible, really, to get any idea of what the salchow looks like by studying one or more photographs. So we'll have to settle for the next best thing: a diagram of the jump and the manner in which you must skate to enter it correctly. You will come to know the salchow's beauty and the movements involved in it by watching it being performed by fellow skaters—and then by performing it yourself.

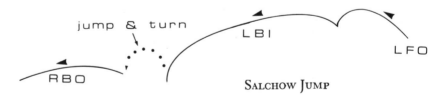

SALCHOW JUMP

Just as with the salchow, all the freestyle movements—from spins to jumps—require that you skate along the ice in a certain way beforehand so that you can enter them correctly. Your coach will show you the best entry routes, just as he will show you how to maneuver around the rink between the various movements. The movements, of course, cannot come right on top of each other, nor should they follow each other too closely. The first is a physical impossibility, while the second is confusing to watch. Your maneuvers in between will give you the time to prepare for each new spin, pivot, or jump, and the time to set each apart from the other so that each will stand out clearly for all to see. Further, they will "round out" your freestyle program, blending your whole performance into a harmonious whole.

There. You've now met the school figures and the basic freestyle movements. The rest is up to you. Ahead lies hard work and the deep satisfaction of developing your figure skating skills and meeting the challenge of competition. Here's hoping that you'll soon be on your way to your first championship.

TEN

For Fun and Competition: Variety on Ice

In this, our last chapter, we are going to talk about three specialized areas of ice skating. They are called specialized areas because they are known to appeal only to certain types of skaters, with the first inviting participants who want a body-contact sport, the second attracting those who wish to work with a partner, and the third beckoning to all who enjoy speed more than anything else.

Because they appeal only to certain skaters, the three have never won as many enthusiasts as have general and figure skating. But they are nevertheless enjoyed by thousands of participants and spectators. By the time you have finished reading this chapter, one or another of the trio may have captured you as a new supporter.

The areas are as different from one another as can be. Together, they serve to round out the variety of fun and challenge to be found on the ice. They are: ice hockey, ice dancing, and speed skating.

Let's now look at each in turn.

ICE HOCKEY

Ice hockey has long been known as Canada's national sport. Recognized as one of the fastest and roughest of team games, it is also played in Western and Eastern Europe, the Soviet Union, Japan, and our own country. Here in the United States, though still most famous for its professional teams, it is enjoying an increasing popularity among amateur players, with many schools, clubs, and rinks across the country now sponsoring teams. Ice hockey has been an official entry in the Olympic Games since 1920.

The game is a relative of field hockey, one of the oldest stick-and-ball sports in the world, a competition invented by the Greeks and then passed to the Romans and the early British. The word *hockey* itself is thought to be derived from the French word *hocquet*, which means a shepherd's curved staff. Historians believe that these staffs were the first sticks and clubs used to bat the game ball around the field of play.

The ice version of the sport seems to have been born in the Canada of the eighteenth or nineteenth century, when the children of Scottish settlers devised an informal game called *shinny*. In it, they skated in pursuit of a small stone and tried to send it whizzing across the opponent's goal line with broomsticks. Adults soon took up the game, after which several teams of British soldiers turned it into the formal sport of ice hockey in the 1860s. The soldiers played their first games at Kingston, Ontario. That city is now recognized as the birthplace of today's ice hockey.

Should you go in for the game, you will find yourself a member of a six-man team made up of the following positions: a goalie (or goalkeeper), a right defense, a left defense, a center, a right wing, and a left wing. You will play on a rink with a cagelike goal at either end. Each goal is 6 feet wide and 4 feet high. Using a wooden stick, your job will be to win points for your team by driving a rubber disk, called a *puck*, into your opponent's goal cage, at the same time preventing the opposition from taking control of the puck and scoring against you.

As an amateur, you will likely play on a rink measuring at least 60 feet wide and from 160 to 185 feet long. Should you move to the professional ranks one day, your playing area will expand to 85 feet wide and 200 feet long. In either case, the area will be surrounded by a wooden barrier about 4 feet high, within whose confines you will participate in a game that is divided into 3 20-minute periods that are separated by intermissions of 10 to 15 minutes.

Whether playing as an amateur or a professional, you will use the same equipment: the regulation stick, lightweight but sturdy skates, and a uniform consisting of shorts, jersey, stockings, shoulder and hip pads, knee guards, and heavily padded gloves. Should you become a goalie, one of the most dangerous and difficult positions to play, your equipment will differ somewhat. To protect yourself, you'll wear a heavy body covering with specially constructed shoulder pads and felt arm protectors; heavy thigh pads; cumbersome leg guards that, measuring 10 inches across, stretch from the ankles to well above the knees; and thick gloves, one of which resembles a first baseman's mitt in baseball. As a goalie, you may, too, want to wear a face mask to safeguard yourself against flying pucks.

Additionally, no matter your position, you may be required to wear a helmet—and you will be required to do so if you are in amateur play. Also required by many amateur teams are mouthguards. Pucks have a bad habit of sailing off the ice. It is anything but pleasant to be hit by one when it is whistling along at an estimated 115 miles an hour.

A special word must be said about your skates and stick, both of which are illustrated here.

The skates consist of steel blades set in tubular aluminum frames that are fastened to heelless shoes. The blades are flat along their undersides, but curve upward at the front and back to provide for sudden changes of direction by the player. The boots are made of durable leather, end at about ankle level, and are usually equipped with a hard box toe for protection in the collisions for which hockey is famous.

The stick is made of hard wood and consists of two parts: the handle and the blade. The length of the stick may not exceed 55 inches. The blade may measure no more than 12½ inches long for professionals, and no more than 14¾ inches for amateurs. With the exception of those carried by goalies, all sticks must describe a forty-five-degree angle at the point where the handle joins the blade.

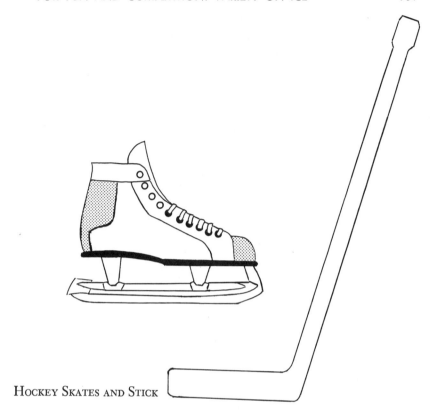

Hockey Skates and Stick

Goalies use sticks whose blades extend out straight from their handles. Their blades measure 3½ inches wide in comparison with the 3-inch widths of those of their teammates.

Now for the game itself: Play begins with what is called the *face-off*. For it, the centers of the opposing teams position themselves in the middle of the rink and wait for the referee to signal for the start of action and drop the puck between them. Once the puck, which measures 3 inches in diameter and 1 inch thick, is on the ice, the centers fight for its possession, the winner then sending it out to surrounding fellow players who, in their turn, try to maneuver it past the opposition's defense and into the goal cage. Throughout, the defenders not only try to prevent a score but also struggle to gain possession of the puck, doing so by blocking or checking the attackers with their sticks and bodies or by intercepting the puck as it skids along the ice. Whenever a team drives the puck into the goal cage, it tallies a point for itself.

A new face-off is used to restart play when a team scores or when a new period begins. Face-offs also occur after play has stopped because the puck has gone out of bounds, a penalty has been called, or the offside whistle has sounded. Once action has commenced, the players may move the puck along with their sticks, skates, bodies, or hands, but they may not score by deliberately kicking or throwing the puck into the goal cage. Nor may they trap the puck with their hands or bodies. Nor may they pick it up and throw it from one to another.

These prohibitions do not apply to the goalie when he is working in the vicinity of his goal cage, in what is known as his "privileged area," a zone that is called the "crease." It measures 2 feet deep by 4 feet wide, and is located directly in front of the goal cage. Here, with but one exception, he may do whatever he thinks necessary to keep the puck from skittering into the cage. He may dive in front of it. He may catch it (this accounts for his first baseman-like mitt). He may deflect it with his stick, his skates, his arms, his body. The exception: He may neither stop nor deflect the puck by throwing his stick at it.

Anyone who has ever played or watched ice hockey will tell you it is one of the roughest games ever devised. Emotions run high, and so penalties are quite commonplace. They are called for such infractions as holding or tripping an opponent, throwing or slashing with a stick, or speaking abusively to an official. Depending on the seriousness of his misconduct, a player may be sent to the penalty box, which is located at the side of the rink, for a few minutes, or may be ejected from the game. In most cases, a substitute is not permitted to play for him while he is cooling his temper in the box. His team is forced to operate at reduced strength.

If you plan to go in for ice hockey, you will need to be ready to skate at high speeds and change direction at will. You will need, too, to learn the arts of blocking, puck interception, and stick handling; this last is the technique of moving the puck swiftly along the ice by tapping it from side to side with the stick. And you will need to be ready to accept all the bumps and bruises that you could ask for in a sport—even more than are suffered in the American game most famous for its body contact, football.

ICE DANCING

Now we go to the opposite extreme—from ice hockey to ice dancing. All that they bear in common is the fact that both take place on the ice. Where the one is all high-speed action and violent contact, the other is all graceful and rhythmic movement.

Ice dancing has long been called figure skating with a partner. Incorporated into it are such figure maneuvers as curves (called *lobes* by ice dancers), spirals, pivots, spins, and jumps. And the range of activity that it offers is quite as wide as that promised by figure skating. On the one hand, just as many pleasure skaters learn a few figures for the sheer fun of it, you and your partner may find a world of enjoyment in doing no more than mastering several basic dance steps or inventing simple dances of your own. On the other, if you are willing to practice the necessary hours, you and your partner may be able to enter USFSA competitive dancing. If sufficiently expert, you may climb from local competitions to a national and even an international level.

For now, let's say that you and your partner are interested in ice dancing simply for the enjoyment involved. There will be nothing to stop you from gracefully skating through a musical number together once you have learned several basic dance positions and steps.

Dance positions are the stances taken by the partners at the beginning of a number or at certain points during its course. In all, eleven are used in ice dancing; but for your purposes, only three will be needed in the beginning, the first of which is the simple *hand-in-hand* position. As the name suggests, the hand of one partner is held in the hand of the other partner as the dancers skate side by side. Should the partners decide to maneuver about each other, they are quite free to change hands.

The next position, which is known as the *waltz* or *closed* position, is quite similar to that used for ordinary ballroom dancing.

The partners stand facing each other, with one skating backward and the other forward. The boy places his right hand against the girl's back at her shoulder blade, while the girl rests her right hand on the boy's shoulder. The left arms are extended to the side, with the hands clasped and the elbows easily bent.

You may alter this position to the *open* or *foxtrot* position. Here the partners simply turn slightly away from each other so that both are able to skate in the same direction.

Finally, there is the *open Kilian* position. The partners stand side by side, with the boy on the left, while both face in the same direction. The boy places his right hand on the girl's right hip, and she holds it pressed there with her right hand. The left arms are extended to the side and slightly forward, with the girl's left hand held by the boy's. This position is chiefly used in a dance known as the *Dutch Waltz*, and may be reversed so that the boy is standing on the girl's right.

The waltz and Kilian positions are shown here in the illustration. The skaters on the left are demonstrating the Kilian, while those on the right have assumed the waltz position.

Now for a few simple dance steps: As you and your partner skate together, try first the simple *cross step forward*. While gliding along on one foot or the other, do no more than bring your free leg forward, cross it in front of your skating leg, and then allow the free blade to run easily on the ice alongside your skating foot, holding it there for several beats of the music.

Then, for a bit of variation, try the *cross step behind*. Again, as you are gliding, cross your legs, but this time place the free leg behind the skating leg.

The *forward chasse* is another easily mastered dance step. Let's say that you are gliding on your left foot, with the right foot extended gracefully to the rear. Bring your right foot forward and place it on the ice alongside the left. Now raise your left foot just off the ice and ride on your right for a few beats, after which the left foot returns to the ice and the right moves back to thrust you into a new stroke. The movement, though as simple as can be to perform, is quite graceful when skated in time to music.

WALTZ AND KILIAN POSITIONS

Once you've tried the chasse, you'll be able to advance to the *forward progressive,* a very similar step. To begin, glide on your left foot, with your right extended to the rear. Carry your right foot forward and lower it to the ice parallel to but just slightly ahead of your left—actually, at a point that will set your right heel about level with your left toes. After the right foot has been held in this position for an appropriate number of beats, send it again to the rear in a stroking action that will propel you along on your left blade.

Finally, you can give the *slide chasse* a try. Once again, glide on your left blade with your right foot to the rear. And again, bring the right foot forward and place it on the ice alongside its companion. Last, shift your weight to the right skate and let your left leg come forward and rise from the ice. Lift the skate no more than a few inches from the surface while keeping the leg above straight and the toes nicely pointed.

All the above steps have been described while you have been gliding on your left blade. All, of course, can be reversed so that they are executed while gliding on the right blade.

Using any of the dance positions to get yourself started, you will now be able to invent simple dances of your own. Into them you will be able to work curves, circles, straight-line skating, pivots, and even jumps. The dance steps can then be blended into the various maneuvers. For instance, you will find that you can easily and interestingly "interrupt" your circles and curves with any step from the cross step forward to the slide chasse.

The positions and steps that we have talked about are among the simpler to be found in ice dancing. They will serve you well for pleasure skating, but, should you decide to enter competitive dancing, you will need to learn many other positions and steps. Competition for you will be much the same as it is for the single figure skater; as he must perform the school figures, you will be called upon to skate certain compulsory dances; and, as he is permitted to skate a freestyle program, you will be allowed to present a program of what is called *free dancing*—that is, a program of your own invention.

And you will be judged just as he is. Your scoring marks will depend on the difficulty of the dance routine, the technical skill that you reveal, and the personal style with which you perform.

Finally, along with the figure skater, you will need a coach if you hope to enter competition. Without his watchful eye, the chance is too great for errors to creep into your routines and movements. He will introduce you to the various positions and steps and will guide you through your rehearsals of the compulsory dances. There are now twenty-two such dances used in competition, all of which are diagramed in *The USFSA Rulebook*.

If you are interested in working with a partner but do not wish to pursue ice dancing, you may wish to look into *pairs skating*. In pairs skating, couples perform various freestyle figure movements and sometimes incorporate dance steps into their programs. Incidentally, ice dancing and pairs skating are so similar that, in some areas, you will hear their names used synonymously, with one meaning exactly the same as the other.

Speed Skating

Is racing for you? Would you like to crank yourself up to a speed of about thirty miles an hour at times? Or average twenty-four miles an hour over a long stretch?

If so, you'll take speed skating right to your heart. Along with skiing, it has long been recognized as the fastest sport in which man moves under his own power. Today, as in years past, it is both a leisure-time activity and a formal sport. As people have done since the days when skates were animal bones tied to the feet, you can engage in informal races with friends or against the clock; informal speed skating is seen regularly on outdoor ponds and during special periods at many rinks. Or, following a tradition that was begun when the world's first recorded ice race was run in the England of 1814, you can participate in formal competition at local, national, and international levels.

Though you may skate any distance you please in a leisure-time race, formal competition is divided into specific distances and is run in one of two styles. The distances, which range from fifty yards to five miles, are designated in meters and are divided into the following events: five hundred meters, one thousand meters, fifteen hundred meters, three thousand meters, five thousand meters, and ten thousand meters. Separate races are held for men and for women.

The two styles in which the races are run are the *American* and the *European*. In the American-style race, several contestants are

SPEED SKATE

pitted against one another and, as in track competition, the winner is the first man across the finish line. The European style sets the racers against the clock. Skaters circle the track, with the man recording the best time being judged the winner.

No matter what the style of race, all equipment used in speed work is light in weight so that nothing will impede the swiftness of the skater. The costume fits snugly and is without any frills that would contribute to wind resistance. As for the skates, their boots are made of a lightweight but tough leather, and their blades of a fine-quality steel cut to a width of about one thirty-second inch.

The length of the blade is the most distinctive feature of the speed skate. It measures up to seventeen inches for long races, and is usually just under fifteen inches for shorter runs. The length is needed so that the skater will be able to move along as swiftly as possible by gripping much ice with each stroke.

At one time, all speed blades were flat along their underside from front to back. In recent years, however, many have been cut with a radius similar to—but slighter than—that of the figure blade. The radius has proven of particular value on short race courses. It helps the skater get easily through the curves repeatedly encountered at either end of the conventional oval track.

As with any other type of skating, a number of techniques are advised for successful speed work. Some are best used in long races, while others are suggested for short hauls. To introduce you to the sport and to help you on your way to your first race, here are a few general tips:

At the Starting Line

Depending much on personal preference and the type of race to be run, there are several ways in which a skater can position himself at the starting line. One of the best and most commonly used stances, as is shown in the illustration here, sets your skates at an angle to the starting line and enables you to propel yourself forward swiftly when the race begins.

To take the position, set yourself so that you are facing in the direction in which you are to skate. Bend your knees and place your

L

R

STARTING STANCE

skates at about forty- to forty-five-degree angle to the line. Let your left leg be ahead of your right, with the toe of your left skate right on the starting line and your right skate about eighteen inches behind. Lean slightly forward, eyes straight ahead. In all, as one instructor has put it, you should give the appearance of a tightly coiled spring.

At the sound of the starting gun—or the command "Go"—spring across the starting line by thrusting yourself forward hard with your right skate. Let your body now bend low. Swing your arms from side to side to help yourself gather momentum. As you lunge forward, do not glide on the left blade. Rather, with feet well apart and legs driving hard, take several steps to gather speed. Keep the steps low to the ice, however, so that you will have no chance to slow down between them. Work yourself gradually into a thrust-and-glide stroke.

In short races, you will want to shoot forward very fast and develop as much speed as you can in the briefest time possible. In longer races, you can employ a somewhat slower start, beginning with gliding strides and then smoothly gathering speed.

On the Straightaway

Very soon after breaking away from the starting line, you will pass through the first turn and enter the track's straightaway area. By the time you are on the straightaway, you should be thrusting and gliding, with your shoulders weaving rhythmically from side to side so that one is always well over the forward knee. Your strokes should be as powerful as you can make them, and the intervening glides should be long. Now—and throughout the race—you should continue holding your body bent low, for it then offers the least surface for wind resistance.

If you are in a race of one thousand meters or more, you should discontinue swinging your arms once you are on the straightaway. In the one-thousand-meter race, the left hand is placed against the small of the back, while the right arm remains free to swing. In races beyond one thousand meters, both hands are clasped at the small of the back.

On the Curve

Many beginning racers feel that they must hurry their strokes on the track curves if they are not to lose speed. No such acceleration is necessary if you are in a long race of the European style.

Your basic job in a distance European event is to set a pace that can be successfully sustained all the way to the finish line. Accelerating only when necessary, you should hold steadily to the pace, whether you are on the straightaway or the curve. The speed acquired on the straightaway can be maintained through the curve if you remain bent low, lean well to the inside of the curve, and continue stroking steadily by passing your right foot in front of your left and then sending the left to the rear in a thrusting action.

Correct body lean on the curve is vital. It should be made all in the usual "one piece." If the lean is insufficient or made with the pelvis thrust out and away from the curve, then your strokes will weaken and you can count on a loss of speed.

In a short race, or near the end of an American-style distance event, you may need to pick up speed on the curve to stay with or move ahead of the pack. If so, you will need to sprint through the curve, doing so by turning your body slightly to the side and then traveling with your blades at right angles to the border of the track. As one instructor has described it, you will look as if you are running sideways. Your right leg will be continuously thrown across the front of your left, and your left will fly to the rear in a series of thrusting actions.

When skating curves in a European-style distance event, you should hold your arms as they are on the straightaway. For the sprinting action, they may swing free to add to your momentum and to steady your balance.

Though it is without violent body contact, speed skating is quite as strenuous a sport as ice hockey. It demands the utmost stamina of all participants. In particular, your wind must be good, and your legs must be in tip-top shape. For a winter of racing, conditioning should begin no later than in late summer or early autumn, and should consist of a well-balanced diet, a daily routine of calisthenics, and a program of long walks and runs in rolling countryside.

With such a training regimen, you will be in fine physical and mental condition when the first ice puts in an appearance. Then out to the starting line you can go with the confidence and the stamina necessary for a racing win.

A Final Note

In this book, we have talked together about many topics—all the way from the first strokes taken by any skater to the intricate movements of the figure skater, the hockey player, the ice dancer, and the speed racer.

It is hoped that you found all the topics interesting and valuable. If you have yet to try the ice for the first time, may they hasten the day when you slip into a pair of skates. If you are already a skater, may they help to improve your skills or open the door to new and fascinating ice activities in which you will find great pleasure and challenge.

Only two things now remain to be said:

GOOD LUCK IN YOUR SKATING. HAVE FUN.

Index

EDWARD F. DOLAN, JR., was born and educated in California, where he and his family live at present. He has lived in the state most of his life. After serving in the 101st Airborne Division during World War II, he was chairman of the Department of Speech and Drama at Monticello College, Alton, Illinois, for three years. While writing books for young people, he spent seven years as a free-lance writer in radio and television, and was a teacher for some years after that. His first book was published in 1958, and he has averaged a book a year since then, while continuing to do free-lance magazine writing and editorial work. For the past ten years, Mr. Dolan has also owned and operated a small publishing company, which produces school materials for mentally retarded children.